DRAUGHTSMAN CIVIL SECOND YEAR MCQ

OBJECTIVE QUESTION ANSWERS

MANOJ DOLE

Digitization is the need of the time. In the future, training in industrial training institutes will need to be conducted using online internet to make training more convenient and easy. E-books containing a set of MCQ questions will be made available to the trainees as they need to be more accustomed to the multiple choice questions MCQ to prepare for the online exams taking place in their industrial training institutes.

With all these factors in mind, Mr. Manoj Madhukar Dole Instructor, Industrial Training Institute, Satara, has written books according to the new annual system and NSQF-5 syllabus. And they've created theoretical mobile apps and blogs to make training easier, and made all these educational materials available for download on the world famous websites Google Play Store, Amazon and Apple Book Store.

The books were published by Hon'ble Joint Director Shri Rajendra Ghume Saheb Regional Office of Vocational Education and Training, Pune on 9/1/2019, at this time Shri Prakash Saigavkar Saheb Principal Government Industrial Training Institute Aundh Pune, Shri Tukaram Misal Saheb Principal Govt. Q. Sanstha Satara, Shri Sachin Dhumal Saheb District Vocational Education and Training Officer Satara, Shri Yatin Pargaonkar Saheb Principal Govt. Q. Sanstha Kolhapur, Shri Vikas Teke Saheb Inspector Vocational Education and Training Regional Office Pune, Palekar Foods Products Pvt. Ltd. Entrepreneurial Chairman of Satara Mr. Nilkanthrao Palekar Saheb, Chairman of Hira Foods Mr. Ibrahim Baba Tamboli Saheb, Mrs. Shalmali Pawar Headmaster Government Technical School Center Satara and other dignitaries were present on the occasion.

Contents

Prologue

Draughtsman Civil Second Year MCQ is a simple e-Book for ITI Engineering Course Draughtsman Civil, Revised NSQF Syllabus in 2022, Draughtsman Civil. It contains objective questions with underlined & bold correct answers MCQ covering all topics including all about the latest & Important about Single storied building plan in traditional drawing.Knowledge and application of Computer Aided Drafting.Workspace creating drawing using toolbars, commands, and menus.Plotting drawing from CAD. 2D drafting of Doors, Windows, hand railing, wash basin, and plumbing joints. Preparing library folders by creating blocks of regularly used items. Preparation of a sanction plan of double storied RCC flat roof residential building using CAD. Preparation of a drawing of public building by framed structure using CAD. Preparation of Bar bending schedule. Drawing of different steel structure joints using CAD. Detail drawing of sanitary fittings and sewerage arrangements using CAD. Detail and sectional drawing of Roads, Bridges, culverts, railway tracks and embankment, Dams, Barrages, Weir and cross drainage works using CAD, schematic diagram of hydro electric project using CAD, Estimating and Cost analysis of different types of buildings and structures, preparation of map using Total Station and location of station point using GPS are being performed as part of practical training, and lots more.

We add new question answers with each new version. Please email us in case of any errors/omissions. This is arguably the largest and best e-Book for All engineering multiple choice questions and answers.

Foreword

Vocational education and training is imparted through the Department of Vocational Education and Training through the Department of Business Education and Business Practical to supply multi-skilled artisans in line with the rapidly growing demand in the industrial sector in the 21st century. All the occupations within the institutions are important, as the trainees from these occupations develop multi-skills as per the demands of the industry.

with the noble intention of making available MCQ e-books suitable for all businesses, considering that all the examinations in all the industries in the industrial sector are conducted online and include MCQ method questions. Mr. Manoj Madhukar Dole has written a very good e-book on MCQ method as per the new annual syllabus. This e-book will definitely be a guide for all the trainees, trainee candidates, training instructors and others concerned.

The author of the book is Mr. Manoj Madhukar Dole, Instructor Gov. ITI Satara has 17 years of training experience. Written as a new annual pattern, this e-book incorporates modern digital QR Code technology to understand the layout, simple language, and simple syntax, diagrams and videos for each subject. So I am sure that this e-book will definitely be useful for in-depth study and exam practice. The work they have done is certainly commendable.

Mr. Tukaram Misal

Principal Government Industrial Training Institute Satara.

Foreword

Preface

DGET New Delhi and CSTARI Kolkata have been implementing an annual pattern for all businesses in ITI since the August 2018 session. The examination system will also be changed and it will be online from this year and since all the questions are of Objective Type (MCQ), the trainees are in dire need of in-depth study. It is with this in mind that we are delighted to present the books based on the old NIMI pattern and a complete overview of the new annual pattern, and we hope that these books will be a guide for all business directors and trainees. Is.

For writing these books, Johar Awate Saheb, Principal of ITI Akluj. Former Principal of ITI Satara Saigavkar Saheb, Assistant Director Shri Chandrakant Dhekne Saheb Regional Office of Vocational Education and Training, Pune, District Vocational Education and Training Officer Sachin Dhumal Saheb and Headmaster Government Technical School Kendra Shalmali Pawar Madam and son Adhiraj Dole, mother Kusum Dole, I am very grateful to my father Madhukar Dole and wife Ashwini Dole for their special guidance and cooperation from time to time.

Also, in a very short period of time, the book was reviewed by Shri Rajendra Ghume Saheb, Joint Director, Vocational Education and Training Regional Office, Pune, for his invaluable time in publishing the book. I am sincerely grateful for their feedback.

I am grateful to the Instructor of ITI Satara for there continuous support from the very beginning of writing the book.

From this book, I consider myself blessed to have shared my thoughts on e-learning with you. I will not claim that this book is perfect, because considering the perfection, this book is an attempt and is in its infancy. They will be valuable for improvement if they are tested and suggested.

Manoj Dole
Dated 9/1/2019

Acknowledgements

The industrial training and theoretical examination system of our industrial training institutes and these changes have been accepted by the craft instructors and the trainees. Theoretical examinations conducted in your industrial training institutes are also conducted online. Since these examinations are of multiple choice MCQ method, the trainees will need to get more practice of such questions.

With all these considerations in mind, Mr. Manoj Madhukar, Director, Dole Crafts, Katari Industrial Training Institute, Satara, has done a thorough study and with his diligent work and added his keen intellect, according to the new annual system and NSQF-5 syllabus, e-book of Katari and other machine trades. -Book) and they have created mobile apps and blogs on theoretical topics to make training easier and have made all these educational materials available for download on the world famous websites Google Play Store, Amazon and Apple Book Store. Training has been made easier by creating a print version and using advanced techniques like QR Code.

All these educational materials will definitely be a guide for all the trainees for in-depth study and for the craft instructors and other concerned who are imparting vocational training.

CHAPTER ONE

Draughtsman Civil Second Year QR Code Images

Download App
Online Test Exam
ITI Books
AutoCAD CAM
JOB & Apprentice
Online Theory
Computer Course
Trading Course
CNC Course
MSCIT Course
Shopping Business
Internet Business
Web Designing
Online Services
Top Sportsmans
Indian Army
Freedom Fighters
Top Scientists
Social Reformers
Motivational Speaker
Top Richest People
Join WhatsApp Group
Join Facebook Group
Like Facebook Page
PAN / Adhar / Licence Passport

AutoCAD Command Shortcut Keys

CTRL+Q Exit public consciousness
CTRL+R Remove ornamentation
CTRL+S Save as Stainless Steel
CTRL+SHFT+S Save as a better design (ie. Titanium)
CTRL+T Toggles Talent (requires administrative access)
CTRL+V Value Engineer (reduces scale by 78%)
CTRL+SHFT+V Pastes data from ArchRecord as Block
CTRL+X Begin unpaid Furlough
CTRL+Y Repeats last award winning design
CTRL+Z Speed dial Zaha Hadid
CTRL+ZZZ Sleep (not applicable)
CTRL+[Cancels current schedule
CTRL+\ Cancels current budget
CTRL+ANGST+DEL (no action)

F1 Displays Help wanted sign in café window
F2 Toggles all text to Helvetica
F3 Toggles Oh-SNAP
F4 Toggles MODERNISM
F5 Toggles ISOLATION
F6 Toggles CORBUSIER
F7 Toggles IRRELEVANT GRID
F8 Toggles ORTHO MODE (should always be on)
F9 Toggles POSTMODERNISM (should always be off)
F10 Toggles NORWAY
F11 Toggles ARROGANCE

AutoCAD Command Shortcut Keys

ALT+F8 Delete detail
ALT+F11 Add white
CTRL+1 Simplify Palette
CTRL+2 Remove Interior Design Palette
CTRL+3 Complicate Construction Process
CTRL+4 Add 4 extraneous sheets
CTRL+5 Remove Client's color Palette
CTRL+6 Remove Client's wife's color Palette (must press hard)
CTRL+7 Markup Set for interns (with only circles and question marks)
CTRL+A Selects objects in drawing that aren't really needed
CTRL+B Sends resume to B.I.G.
CTRL+SHIFT+B Shifts blame to Consultants
CTRL+C Copies angst to Clipboard
CTRL+SHFT+C Copies angst to Clipboard with Base Point (ie. Finland)
CTRL+D Delete relevance
CTRL+E Cycles through design ideologies
CTRL+F Flatten all roofs
CTRL+G Insert 9-square Grid
CTRL+H Insert Awesomeness
CTRL+L Adds "Le" in front of all nouns
CTRL+K Justify design concept
CTRL+L Left justify design concept
CTRL+M Less and/or more
CTRL+N Insert new idea (bills client for additional time required)
CTRL+O Opens ArchDaily.com
CTRL+P Prints unemployment check

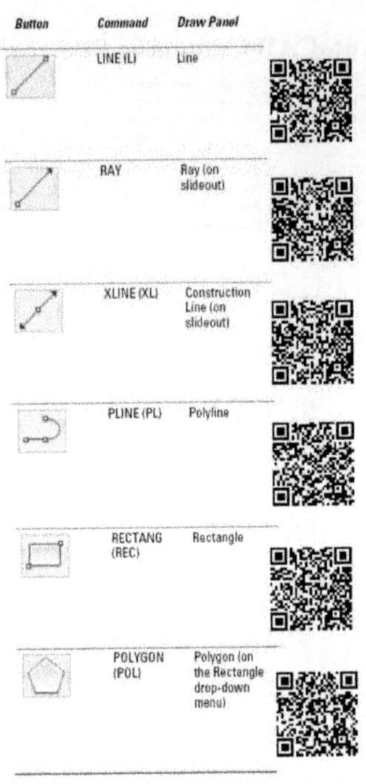

Button	Command	Draw Panel
	LINE (L)	Line
	RAY	Ray (on slideout)
	XLINE (XL)	Construction Line (on slideout)
	PLINE (PL)	Polyline
	RECTANG (REC)	Rectangle
	POLYGON (POL)	Polygon (on the Rectangle drop-down menu)

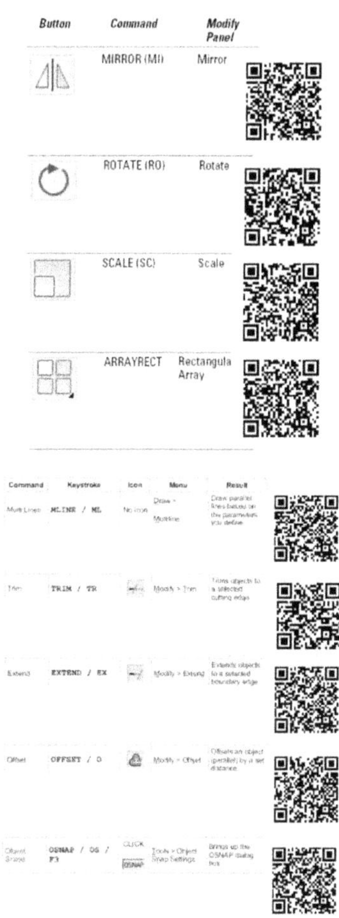

Button	Command	Modify Panel
	MIRROR (MI)	Mirror
	ROTATE (RO)	Rotate
	SCALE (SC)	Scale
	ARRAYRECT	Rectangula Array

Command	Keystroke	Icon	Menu	Result
Multi Lines	MLINE / ML	No icon	Draw > Multiline	Draw parallel lines based on the parameters you define
Trim	TRIM / TR		Modify > Trim	Trims objects to a selected cutting edge
Extend	EXTEND / EX		Modify > Extend	Extends objects to a selected boundary edge
Offset	OFFSET / O		Modify > Offset	Offsets an object (parallel) by a set distance
Object Snaps	OSNAP / OS / F3	CLICK OSNAP	Tools > Object Snap Settings	Brings up the OSNAP dialog box

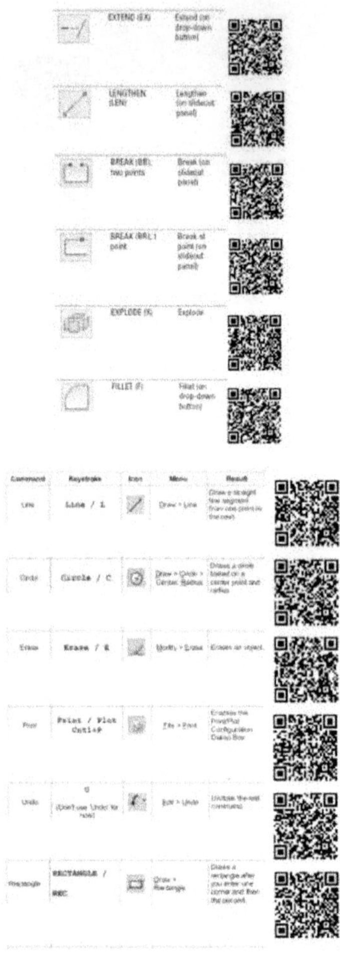

Icon	Command	Location
	EXTEND (EX)	Extend (on drop-down button)
	LENGTHEN (LEN)	Lengthen (on slideout panel)
	BREAK (BR), two points	Break (on slideout panel)
	BREAK (BR), 1 point	Break at point (on slideout panel)
	EXPLODE (X)	Explode
	FILLET (F)	Fillet (on drop-down button)

Command	Keystroke	Icon	Menu	Result
Line	Line / L		Draw > Line	Draw a straight line segment from one point to the next
Circle	Circle / C		Draw > Circle > Center, Radius	Draws a circle based on a center point and radius
Erase	Erase / E		Modify > Erase	Erases an object.
Print	Print / Plot Ctrl+P		File > Print	Enables the Print/Plot Configuration Dialog Box
Undo	U (Don't use 'Undo' for now)		Edit > Undo	Undoes the last command.
Rectangle	RECTANGLE / REC		Draw > Rectangle	Draws a rectangle after you enter one corner and then the second.

Button	Command	Modify Panel
	ERASE (E)	Erase
	MOVE (M)	Move
	COPY (CO or CP)	Copy
	STRETCH (S)	Stretch
	ARRAYPOLAR	Polar Array
	ARRAYPATH	Path Array
	ARRAYEDIT	Edit Array (on slideout panel)
	OFFSET (O)	Offset
	TRIM (TR)	Trim (on drop-down button)

Move / copy
Rotate
Scale
Mirror
Move and rotate
Rotate with two centers
Trim / extend
Trim / extend two
Lengthen / shorten
Stretch
Bevel
Round corner

CHAPTER TWO

Draughtsman Civil Second Year MCQ

1] Which is the latest version of AutoCAD software?
a) 2016
b) 2017
c) 2018
d) 2019

2] Which key is used to obtain properties palette in AutoCAD?
a) Control+1
b) Control+2
c) Control+3
d) Control+4

3] AutoCAD was first released in the year]
a) 1858
b) 1966
c) 1898
d) 1982

4] How many units are available in AutoCAD?
a) 4
b) 5
c) 7
d) 6

441] Which mode allows the user to draw 90° straight lines]
a) Osnap
b) Ortho
c) Linear
d) Polar tracking

5] To obtain parallel lines, concentric circles and parallel curves; __________ is used.

a) Array
b) Fillet
c) Copy
d) Offset

6] The default grid spacing in both X and Y directions is]

a) 10
b) 20
c) 5
d) 15

7] How many workspaces are available in AutoCAD?

a) 2
b) 4
c) 3
d) 5

8] Scale command can be accessed easily by typing]

a) SL
b) S
c) SC
d) C

9] Which command is used to divide the object into segments having predefined length?

a) Divide
b) Chamfer
c) Trim
d) Measure

10] How many grip points does a circle have?

a) 5
b) 4
c) 3
d) 2

11] When drawing in 2D, what axis do you NOT work with?

A] X
B] Y
C] Z
D] WCS

12] The primary difference between the Model tab and the Layout tab(s) is _____.

A] the Model tab is used for drawing in 3D and a Layout is used for drawing in 2D

B] <u>the Model tab is where you create the drawing and a Layout tab represents the sheet that you will plot or print on</u>

C] the color of the background

D] the Model tab displays the drawing you are copying from and the Layout tab is where you lay out the new drawing

13] Which of the following is NOT a property of an object

A] Line weight

B] <u>Measure</u>

C] Hyperlink

D] Elevation

14] Which command convert discrete objects in polyline

A] Union

B] Subtract

C] Join

D] Polyline

15] To print the entire project, you will choose to regulate what to plot

A] Display

B] Extends

C] <u>Limits</u>

D] Window

16] What is the usefulness of viewports

A] <u>Allows us to see the screen or on paper different views of the same project</u>

B] Give us the ability to see projects have become a newer version of AutoCAD from our

C] We can make a change in one part of the plan, without affecting the rest

D] None of the above

17] What is the difference between the Scale command from the command Zoom

A] Scale for single object, while the Zoom whole plan

B] No difference

C] H Scale can grow / shrink a shape up 10 times, while the Zoom has no limits

D] H Scale changes the size of objects, while the Zoom changes the visibility of the project

455] When to fix a block attribute

A] Before you fix the block

B] When I make the block

C] After fix the block

D] No matter the number

456] What you cannot create from the command Offset

A] Vertical straight

B] Concentric circles

C] Three parallel lines

D] Parallel arcs

457] By what symbol shows the snap point to the closest point

A] with circles and dots in the center

B] With two triangle

C] With three orthogonal

D] With Diamond

458] Which state grid is use to design perspective

A] Parametric

B] Isometric

C] Pro-optic

D] Rectangular

459] If I want to draw a line in the direction 07]30 (local time) will give an angle

A] -135 degrees

B] 270 degrees

C] -225 degrees

D] None of the above

460] When in absolute Cartesian coordinates have points A (10.8) and B (6.5), then to make a line from A -> B with relative polar coordinates will write

A] @ -5 <36.88

B] @ 4 <30

C] @ 5 <216.88

D] @ 3 <60

461] What is the minimum allowable number of layers in a drawing

A] 0

B] 5

C] 1

D] 2

462] Which of the following is not a keyboard shortcut of AutoCAD?

A] Ctrl + P

B] Alt + F4

C] Ctrl + F4

D] Alt + B

463] Why do we have 16,7 M colors in RGB

A] Because so one can distinguish man

B] since this is the limit of graphics cards

C] For each color we have 256 shades and colors combination third

D] Because we want compatibility between PC and Macintosh

464] What setting gradient allows us to fill an open area?

A] Gap

B] Tolerance

C] Transparency

D] Open

465] What are the various options from left to right and the opposite direction?

A] Choose a different category of objects

B] select objects according to their color

C] Select objects according to their position

D] No difference

466] Which is corresponded to zoom mouse wheel?

A] Zoom in / zoom out

B] pan & scan

C] extents / all

D] scale

467] What command allows us to select objects based on some status?

A] Properties

B] Qselect

C] Pselect

D] Attributes

468] How to make a random line with an angle of 40 degrees to the x axis

A] will write 0 <40

B] will write 2 <40

C] will write 3<40

D] will write 4 <40

469] Which of the following file extensions cannot open the AutoCAD

A] dwg

B] dxf

C] dot

D] dws

470] A surveyor with a headband to measure the dimensions of a site, he make measurements by

A] No one method

B] Related Cartesian coordinates

C] Absolute polar coordinates

D] None of the above

471] What is the command used for Plagiostomi angle?

A] Chamfer

B] Fillet

C] Offset

D] Mirror

472] When should I use the Block Editor

A] To write text block

B] To fix outer block

C] To fix dynamic block

D] To store it in another version of AutoCAD

473] If the scheme that stores will be opened in AutoCAD 2006 then you must save it in

A] AutoCAD 2004 dwg

B] AutoCAD 2006 dwg

C] AutoCAD 2007 dwg

D] None of the above

474] Print scale 1]50 means that

A] The draft is 50 times less expensive than the original

B] A 3 cm corresponds to half a meter

C] A measure corresponds to 50 cm

D] None of the above

475] What do the letters UCS

A] Uniform Calculator System

B] United CAD System

C] Universal CAD Settings

D] Universal Coordinate System

476] What is the difference of two regular 8-gonon, which is one inscribed and another circumscribed circle

A] No difference
B] different opening angles
C] different side length
D] different crowd sides

477] If during the CCW measurement result gives an angle 135 degrees, the same CW angle measured is

A] 225 degrees
B] -135 degrees
C] -225 degrees
D] 135 degrees

478] What does associative hatch

A] Monitors the changes in shape that fills
B] Relates to the other hatch plan
C] Both of the above
D] None of the above

479] What is the difference between command Plot and Print

A] plot command prints only big plans
B] The plot command for CNC (CAM)
C] No difference
D] print command can print up to A3 size paper

480] If you change the scale list a project that I have started from 1]50 1]10 then

A] You will have to start over
B] You should not raise the objects already exist (scale) by 5
C] You will not need to change anything in hitherto methodology
D] should be converted into new items that will add based on the new scale

481] Which of the following is NOT a unit of length measurement?

A] Yards
B] Parsecs

C] Microns
D] Grads

482] What does the command Wblock
A] Warp-speed block
B] Write block
C] Window block
D] Wide-area block

483] Where should you pay attention when you are working with autocad commands?
A] Drawing area
B] Status bar
C] Tool bars
D] Command window

484] Polar coordinates are used mostly for drawing______
A] Arc
B] Ellipse
C] Angular lines
D] None of the above

485] How many SNAP points does an object have?
A] 1
B] 4
C] 5
D] Depend on object

486] How many points do you need to define for the rectangle command?
A] One
B] Two
C] Three
D] Four
487] How many AutoCAD objects are in a rectangle?
A] One
B] Two
C] Three
D] Four

488] How will you deselect an object while you are selecting set of objects?
A] Ctrl+ click on the object to be removed
B] Shift + Click on the object to be removed
C] Alt + Click on the object to be removed
D] None of the above

489] How long will a line from 0,5 to 5,5 be ________
A] 10 units
B] 5 units
C] 15 units
D] None of the above
490] Objects are rotated around the
A] Bottom of the object
B] Base point
C] Center of the object
D] Origin
491] The origin of a drawing is at
A] 0,0
B] 1,0
C] 0,1
D] 1,1
492] How would you select set of objects in a drawing?
A] By a crossing window drawn from right to left
B] By a crossing window drawn left to right
C] Shift+ clicking on the objects
D] None of the above
493] Fillet command can be used to obtain__________
A] Sharp corners
B] Round corners
C] Both of the above
D] None of the above
494] A polar array creates new objects_____
A] In a grid pattern
B] In a circular pattern
C] In a straight line
D] All of the above
495] How many layers a drawing should have?

A] 1

B] 2

C] As many as depending on the complexity

D] None of the above

496] Scaling objects make them______

A] Smaller

B] Bigger

C] Either smaller or bigger

D] None of the above

1 Which command do you click for drawing line in Auto CAD

A Circle

B Line

C Arc

D Undo

Answer- B

2 From which menu bar do you get 'Line' command

A Layout

B Modify

C Draw

D Insert

Answer- C

4 Which option of command do you have to pick for creating a circle based on two end

points of the diameter

A 2P

B 3P

C TTR Centre

D Radius

Answer- A

5 Which keystroke do you type to use circle

command

A CO

B C

C O

D L

Answer- B

7 What do you mean by 'SER' in Arc command

A Start end radius

B Start end round
C Start easy radius
D Second end radius
Answer- A
10 Which menu bar has erase command in auto CAD
A Draw
B Modify
C Layer
D Setting
Answer- B
11 What is the keystroke for erase command in auto CAD
A ER
B E
C ES
D EL
Answer- B
13 What is the shortcut key for 'undo' command in auto CAD
A Ctrl + R
B Ctrl + Z
C Ctrl + V
D Ctrl + C
Answer- B
14 Which menu tab has undo command in auto CAD
A Draw
B Modify
C Edit
D New
Answer- C
15 What is the alternative command of undo
A Redo
B Erase
C Delete
D Dot
Answer- A
16 From which menu tab do you find 'break'

command in Auto CAD
A Draw
B Edit
C Layer
D Modify
Answer- D
17 What is the keystroke for break command
A B
B BR
C BS
D EX
Answer- B
18 Why do we use 'Break' command in auto
CAD
A To erase the object
B to split the object into two parts
C To extend the object part
D To trim the selected part
Answer- B
2 In which toolbar do you find 'Move'
Command in Auto CAD
A Draw
B New
C Modify
D Edit
Answer- C
3 What is the keystroke for 'Copy' command
in AutoCAD
A CY
B CC
C C
D CO "
Answer- D
4 What is the application of 'Copy' command in AutoCAD
A Multiplication of identical objects on the target points.
B Extend the object
C Move the object
D Repetition of command.

Answer- A

5 'Trim' command in AutoCAD is required for _______ object

A Drawing

B Modifying

C Annotating

D Formatting

Answer- B

6 What is the shortcut key for 'Trim' command

A TR

B TP

C TT

D TK

Answer- A

9 What is fillet command

A Rounding the sharp edge

B Cutting the sharp edge

C Break the corner edge

D Extend the edge

Answer- A

10 What is the shortcut key for 'Fillet' command

A C

B B

C F

D L

Answer- C

11 Which drop down menu contains 'Fillet' command

A Annotate

B Parametric

C Modify

D View

Answer- C

12 What is command prompt of 'Chamfer'

A F

B Cha

C Ex

D L

Answer- B

13 Why do you use 'Chamfer' command
A to bevel the sharp corner
B to break the line
C to radius the two corners
D to trim the two corners
Answer- A
15 What is command prompt of 'Rotate'
A RE
B RO
C R
D XR
Answer- B
16 What is shortcut command of 'Scale'
A SC
B A
C B
D S
Answer- A
17 Which command do you use for enlarging any drawing
A COPY
B SCALE
C ERASE
D ROTATE
Answer- B
18 Which command is represented by the given symbol
A Rectangle
B Offset
C Scale
D Copy
Answer- C
2 Which command prompt is used for insertblock
A J
B I
C L
D C
Answer- B
3 What is the basic use of I/Block for block
A For reusable contents

B For recreatingcontents

C For making object

D For editing contents

Answer- A

4 Which menu bar contains block command

A Insert

B Draw

C Modify

D Dimension

Answer- A

5 What is the shortcut key to make block command

A I

B B

C C

D L

Answer- B

6 Which command is used after making the required object to make block

A Mirror

B Block

C Copy

D Array

Answer- B

7 Which command panel contains 'Hatch' command

A Insert block

B Draw

C Layer

D Modify

Answer- B

8 What is the shortcut of 'Hatch' command

A B

B I

C H

D M

Answer- C

9 What is the use of 'Hatch' command

A To make multiple object

B To fill an enclosed area with a pattern

C To create new close object
D To split the object
Answer- B
11 In which command window do you find gradient
A Block
B Hatch
C Circle
D Array
Answer- B
13 What is the application of array command in Auto CAD
A Distributed copies of selected object in rectangular or circular pattern
B To create deflected object
C To copy object in irregular form
D To create scattered mirror image
Answer- A
14 How many types of array command are there in Auto CAD
A 3
B 2
C 1
D 4
Answer- C
15 What is polar array
A To make multiple copies of an object in circular pattern
B To draw any object in circular pattern
C To hatch any object
D To move any object
Answer- A
16 Which command panel contains array command
A Modify
B Draw
C Dimension
D Drafting Setting
Answer- A
17 What is main advantage of using array command
A It allows you to copy objects in a definite angle and exact no.of copy
B To enlarge the object
C To enclose the boundary of object
D To create mirror image of object

Answer- A

18 What is shortcut of array command

A A

B AR

C B

D C

Answer- B

1 What is a template in AutoCAD

A A file that is already setup for specific application

B A file contains different types of figure

C A command for creating identical object

D A command for making a block

Answer- A

2 A selected template file open in Auto CAD________

A Model space

B Layout space

C Work space

D space

Answer- B

3 Which command is used for opening a template

A New

B Open

C Insert

D Format

Answer- A

4 Where do you click to create a new layer

A Layer properties

B Block

C Scale

D Circle

Answer- A

5 How do layers help

A Layer makes multiple objects

B Layer creates identical objects

C Layers allow to easy control and edit properties of a group of objects

D Layer makes block object

Answer- C

6 Which pull down menu contains layer

A Format
B Draw
C Annotation
D Help
Answer- A
7 What do you find in layer dialogue box among the followings
A Scale
B Line type
C Copy
D Displacement
Answer- B
8 Which sign should you click to disappear the layer from the screen in layer dialogue
box
A On freeze sign
B On bulb
C On lock sign
D On box sign
Answer- B
9 What is the shortcut command of layer
A LA
B L1
C L
D LO
Answer- A
10 What do you mean by 'DIMALINIER' command
A To draw a linear dimension
B To draw an aligned dimension
C To draw dimension for diameter circle
D To draw angular dimension
Answer- A
12 What is the command of dimension for radius for circles or arcs
A QLEADER
B DIMEDIT
C DIMRADIUS
D DIMDIAMETER
Answer- C
13 What command is used for doing own dimension style

A DIEMDIT

B DIMSTYLE

C DIM

D ANGULAR DIMRAIUS

Answer- B

16 Which one of these options pallate is found in Modify Dimension Style dialogue box

A Primary units

B Polar tracking

C By layer

D Format

Answer- A

17 What will be the command prompt to create new dimension style

A DDIM

B DIMEDIT

C QLEADER

D DIM RADIUS

Answer- A

1 What do you mean by 3D

A Four dimension

B Three dimension

C Two dimension

D One dimension

Answer- B

2 What is the advantage of 3D

A Helps to reduce size in design

B Helps you conceptualize design

C Helps to edit work in design

D Helps to print the drawing

Answer- B

3 Which toolbar do you click on Auto CAD window for 3D drawing environment

A Draw

B Modify

C Workspace

D Format

Answer- C

4 Which command panel / ribbon contains 3D primitives in 3D modelling drawing space

A Home

B Solid

C Insert

D View

Answer- B

6 Which one is 3D primitive command among these options

A LINE

B POLYGON

C CIRCLE

D CONE

Answer- D

7 What is the shortcut of Extrude command

A EX

B E

C Ext

D ED

Answer- C

8 In Which direction height of extrusion is measured

A X Direction

B Y Direction

C Z Direction

D XZ Direction

Answer- C

9 What is the shortcut of revolve command

A R

B RE

C REV

D REC

Answer- C

10 Why does the revolve command is used

A To create a solid model

B To create 2D object

C To rotate object

D to move object

Answer- A

11 What is the full form of UCS

Universal Coordinate system
Use co-ordinate system
Usual co-ordinate system
Union co-ordinate system
Answer- B
12 Default origin of UCS is
A World
B Current
C Universal
D Local
Answer- A
13 In which command panel do you find 3D rotate
A Modify
B Draw
C Format
D Insert
Answer- A
14 What is the use 3D rotate command
A Helps to rotate 3D object
B Helps to copy 3D object
C Helps to pull 3D object
D Helps to align 3D object
Answer- A
15 Which ribbon is combined with plot command in Auto CAD window
A Home
B Output
C Layout
D View
Answer- B
16 What is shortcut of print command
A Ctrl + X
B Ctrl + C
C Ctrl + P
D Ctrl + F
Answer- C
17 What is full preview
A Preview the print after plot setting
B Preview of parts drawing

C Properly drawing object

D Perfectly print drawing

Answer- A

18 Which command dialogue box contains preview command

A Plot

B Drafting setting

C Drawing units

D Plotter manager

Answer- A

1] Which of the following is the basic need of a human being?

A] Sheet

B] Shelter

C] Huts

D] Tree

2] Which of the following gives major importance to outside view?

A] Aspect

B] Prospect

C] Grouping

D] Lighting

3] What is the shape of the given plan?

A] Square

B] Rectangle

C] Oblong

D] Circle

4] What is the other name of circulation in the same floor?

A] Horizontal circulation

B] Vertical circulation

C] Zig - Zag circulation

D] Winding circulation

5] Who is having legal interest in land or building?

A] Leaser

B] Mortagee

C] Mortager

D] Owner

6] Which of the following shape of plan makes home compact?

A] Square

B] Rectangle

C] Oblong

D] Circle

7] Which of the following standard should considered in planning?

A] IS codes for planning

B] ISI

C] NBC 2005

D] Local building - Bye laws

8] Who is responsible for providing the legality of the plot?

A] Leaser

B] Mortagee

C] Mortager

D] Owner

9] Which room should be situated near kitchen and drawing?

A] Bed room

B] Living room

C] Dining room

D] Hall

10] Which room is provided for learning and reading in residential building?

A] Drawing room

B] Study room

C] Entertainment room

D] Work room

11] What is the name of the room?

A] Bed room
B] Study room
C] Dining room
D] Multi purpose room
12] How the economy achieved in building?
A] Providing simple elevation
B] Increasing the storey height
C] Increasing steps of stairs
D] Utilizing large sized component
13] What is the name of the useable floor area excluding staircase?
A] Circulation area
B] Carpet area
C] Covered area
D] Plinth area
14] What is the name of the built up area at the floor level?
A] Plinth
B] Plinth area
C] Plinth height
D] Plinth level
15] What is the formula for floor area ratio?
A] (Total area of walls / Total plot area) x 100
B] (Total area of all floors / Total area of walls) x 100
C] (Total area of all floors / Total plot area) x 100
D] (Total plot area / Total area of all floors) x 100
16] What should be the distance between building electric supply mains?
A] 1.0 - 1.8 m

B] 1.0 - 2.0 m

C] 1.2 - 2.0 m

D] 1.5 - 2.0 m

17] What is the minimum scale of which the key plan need to be drawn according to NBC - 2005?

A] 01]50

B] 1]100

C] 1]200

D] 1]400

18] Which plan is approved and sanctioned by competent authority?

A] Approved plan

B] Sanctioned plan

C] Key plan

D] Site plan

19] What is the name of the plan which gives location with respect to neighbourhood boundary in 1]10000?

A] Site plan

B] Key plan

C] Layout plan

D] Approved plan

20] What is the another name of dwelling unit?

A] Row building

B] Residential building

C] Commercial building

D] Educational building

21] What is the name of horizontally sliced building viewed from top?

A] Plan

B] Section

C] Elevation

D] Sectional elevation

22] What is the another name for "Sub-divisional plan"?

A] Key plan

B] Layout plan

C] Sanctioned plan

D] Approved plan

23] What is the maximum number of floors that can be allowed in residential building as per NBC 2005?

A] 2 Floors

B] 3 Floors
C] 4 Floors
D] 5 Floors
24] Which of the following IS code in used for fire safety?
A] IS 1641 - 1960
B] IS 456 - 200
C] IS 291 - 1972
D] IS 10711 - 1984
25] Which of the following is used as escape elements in building for fire safety?
A] Lobbies
B] Strong room
C] Floors
D] Outer walls
26] What is the abbrevation for MOEF?
A] Ministry of Ecology and Forest
B] Ministry of Environment and Federation
C] Ministry of Environment and Forest
D] Ministry of Ecology and
27] Which does forest conservation act was passed?
A] 1992
B] 1980
C] 1972
D] 2000
28] What is the name of the figure given below?

A] Stack effect
B] Wind effect
C] Mechanical effect
D] Artificial effect
29] Which of the following position of door and type of door shutter offer more privacy to room?
A] Centre door - Single shutter

B] Centre door - Double shutter

C] Corner door - Single shutter

D] Corner door - Double shutter

30] Which of the following room in residential building need more air changes per hour, while comparing to bed room in residential building?

A] Drawing room

B] Master bed room

C] Kitchen

D] Hall

31] If the area of the building is same, which of the following building is cheaper compared to single storey?

A] 2 storey building

B] 3 storey building

C] 4 storey building

D] 5 storey building

32] Which of the following is the important advantage of orientation of building?

A] Aesthetic

B] Reduction in energy bills

C] Improved circulations

D] Outdoor projection

33] What is the minimum scale at which a building plan need to be drawn according to NBC 2005?

A] 1]50

B] 1]100

C] 1]200

D] 1]400

34] Which season gives more lighting to the building?

A] Summer

B] Winter

C] Spring

D] Autumn

35] What is the maximum covered area for an Industry?

A] 40% of the site area

B] 50% of the site area

C] 60% of the site area

D] 70% of the site area

36] What is the name of the group institutional building was classified?

A] Group C

B] Group E

C] Group H

D] Group I

37] Which type of building comes in group H?

A] Hazardous

B] Industrial

C] Storage

D] Business

38] What is the name of the part parallel between boundary and the building?

A] Abut line

B] Set back line

C] Plot line

D] Plinth line

39] What is the formula for carpet area?

A] Total plot area - Circulation area

B] Total circulation area - Floor area

C] Total floor area - Circulation area

D] Total area of all floors - Wall area

40] What is the full form of FSI?

A] Floor Site Index

B] Floor Space Index

C] Floor Staircase Index

D] Floor Storey Index

41] How many persons require one wash basin in public buildings?

A] 100

B] 150

C] 175

D] 200

42] Which building provides sleeping and cooking facilities?

A] Institutional building

B] Educational building

C] Residential building

D] Hotel building

43] Which is the important room in a residential building W.R.T NBC 2005?

A] Kitchen

B] Bed room

C] Hall

D] Drawing room

44] What is the normal life period of a residential building with concrete roof according to NBC 2005?

A] 50

B] 75

C] 100

D] 110

45] Which group in which custodial institution comes?

A] Educational building

B] Institutional building

C] Assembly building

D] Business building

46] What is the allowable height of riser in public building W.R.T to NBC 2005?

A] 12 cm

B] 15 cm

C] 17 cm

D] 19 cm

47] Which classification does row building comes in?

A] Public building

B] Residential building

C] Educational building

D] Institutional building

48] What is the lead air charges per hour needed in a restaurant kitchen?

A] 8

B] 10

C] 12

D] 14

49] Which classification of the building have highest F.A.R permissible?

A] Residential building

B] Educational building

C] Institutional building

D] Mercantile building

50] What is the permissible F.A.R for commercial building?

A] 1.5

B] 2

C] 2.5

D] 3

51] Where does laboratories comes in the under ground shopping?

A] Mercantile building

B] Business building

C] Industrial building

D] Educational building

52] What is the basic detail needed for a design engineer, while designing assembly building?

A] Area of plot

B] Number of fixed seats

C] Location of plot

D] Total floor area

53] What is the full form of CPU?

A] Craft Processing Unit (CPU)

B] Code Processing Unit (CPU)

C] Central Processing Unit (CPU)

D] CD Processing Unit (CPU)

54] Which year does first micro processor was invented?

A] 1970

B] 1971

C] 1972

D] 1973

55] What is the name of figure?

A] Mouse

B] Monitor

C] Keyboard

D] Plotter

56] What is the full form of CADD?

A] Computer Aided designing and Drafting

B] Computer Aided Drafting and Drawing

C] Computer Aided Drawing and designing

D] Computer Aided Drawing

57] What is the highest dots per inch (DPI) one can print a

A] 800 dpi

B] 1000 dpi

C] 1200 dpi

D] 1400 dpi

58] What is the full form of GUI?

A] Golden User Installation

B] Graphical User Installation

C] Graphical User Interface

D] Geometrical User Interface

59] What is the name of the tool bar given below?

A] Draw

B] Modify

C] Dimension

D] Visual styles

60] What is the use of function key F3?

A] OSNAP

B] TABLET

C] ISOPLANE

D] SAVE AS

61] Which of the following software is limited for AutoCAD installation?

A] Windows DOS

B] Windows 98

C] Windows 03

D] Windows 10

62] What is the lowest RAM in which AutoCAD 19 will work?

A] 1 GB

B] 2 GB

C] 3 GB

D] 4 GB

63] What is name of the section denoted as 'X'?

A] Product key
B] Auto key
C] Product number
D] Serial number
64] What is the name of the command from the figure given below?

A] Star command
B] Array command
C] Point command
D] Trim command
65] What is the name of the command in the figure given below?

A] Offset

B] Constraction line
C] Multi line
D] P line
66] What is the name of the command in the figure given below?

A] P line
B] M line
C] Spline
D] Poly line
67] What is the full form of UCS?
A] User CAD System
B] User CADD System
C] User Co-ordinate System
D] User Circle System
68] What is the name of the point marked as 'x'?

A] Midpoint of dolar
B] Midpoint of offset
C] Centre point of array
D] Centre point of leader line
69] What is the name of the tool bar given below?

A] Modify weight
B] Line weight
C] Multi line
D] Units
70] What is the name of the tool bar given below?

A] Offset
B] Multi line
C] Line width
D] Line weight
71] Which command has the options given below?

A] Snap
B] Pan
C] Grid
D] Real time
72] What is the name of the tool bar marked as 'x'?

A] Task button
B] Snap button
C] Option button
D] Menu button
73] How this option menu given below opens?

A] Left click
B] Right click
C] Centre click
D] Clicking F1
74] What is the name of the menu bar given below?

A] M text
B] Text
C] Text style
D] Text colour
75] Which shortcut key does the work of ortho?
A] F6
B] F7
C] F8
D] F9
76] Which shortcut key does the work of Redo last action?
A] Ctrl + Z
B] Ctrl + Y
C] Ctrl + C D] Ctrl + X
77] What is the use of shortcut key 'H'?
A] Help
B] B hatch
C] Hatch
D] Hollow block
78] What is the use of the shortcut key 'M Text'?
A] Modify text
B] Move text
C] Multi text D] Menu text
79] What is the use of 'Q' shortcut key?
A] Quit
B] Quick calc
C] Save as
D] "Q" leader
80] Which of the following shortcut keys gives quick calc?

A] Ctrl + 6

B] Ctrl + 7

C] Ctrl + 8 D] Ctrl + 9

81] Which of the following pointing device is cheaper while comparing the digitizer?

A] Key board

B] Puck

C] Mouse

D] Enter key

82] Which of the following commands has one major option?

A] Line

B] M line

C] P line

D] Polygon

83] What is the another name for pre-fabricated structures?

A] Pre-developed structures

B] Modular structures

C] High structures

D] Site fixing structures

84] What is the name of the prefabricating method?

A] Flow method

B] Fixed method

C] Stand method

D] Hand method

85] Which prefabricated method the units of moved to various section for process?

A] Flow method

B] Fixed method

C] Stand method

D] Vehicle method

86] What is the name of the concrete, that are prepared at factory and erected at site?

A] Pre-stressed concrete

B] Post-tensioned concrete

C] Pre-casted concrete

D] Post-casted concrete

87] What is the scale used for prefabricated structure?

A] IS 15913 - 2011

B] IS 15914 - 2011

C] IS 15915 - 2011

D] IS 15916 - 2011

88] What is the minimum distance between centres of any two adjacent rivet holes to the nominal diameter of the rivet is £ 25mm?

A] Nominal diameter +1.0mm

B] Nominal diameter +1.5mm

C] Nominal diameter +2.0mm

D] Nominal diameter +2.5mm

89] What is the first stage of prefabricated structure construction?

A] Testing of raw materials

B] Procurement of raw materials

C] Concrete mix design

D] Reinforcement preparation

90] Which part of the prefabricated building structure aim be constructed at site?

A] Roof slab

B] Foundation

C] Main beams

D] Fillers

91] Which system facilitates assembling of minor elements in conventional construction?

A] Open pre-fab system

B] Partial pre-fab system

C] Full pre-fab system

D] Closed pre -fab system

92] What is the name of assembling structural components at site?

A] Open pre-fab system B] Partial pre-fab system

C] Full pre-fab system

D] Closed pre-fab system

93] Which is the production of housing components using factory mechanisation?

A] Prefabrication

B] Fabrication

C] Construction

D] Production

94] Which system is used with double tee slaps for precast beams and walls?

A] Load bearing
B] Non load bearing
C] Framed structures
D] Foundation
95] Which of the following concrete require transportation for placing?
A] In site concrete
B] Post tensioned concrete
C] Pre cast concrete
D] Pre- stressed concrete
96] Which of the following is the advantage of prefabricated structures?
A] Transportation
B] Need of heavy duty cranes
C] Deformation of joints
D] No need of fastening
97] What is the advantage of prefabricated structure?
A] Transportation
B] No need of heavy duty cranes
C] Firm joints
D] Mass production
98] Which section provide one monotitic action between prefabricated units?
A] Composite
B] Steel
C] Tensile
D] Compression
99] What is the procedure to attain complete action between stem and flange?
A] Laced together
B] Tied together
C] Keyed together
D] Cutted together
100] What is the disadvantage in prefabricated structure?
A] Shorter construction time
B] Financial savings
C] Reduced site disruption
D] Transportation
101] What is the area of playground for 1000 children?
A] 0.10 hectare

B] 0.13 hectare
C] 0.16 hectare
D] 0.20 hectare
102] Which one of the following is the hard land scape?
A] Plantation
B] Types of trees
C] Design of space for people
D] Terrace gardens
103] In which portion of tectonic plates, earthquake generally occurs?
A] Plate boundaries
B] Diversion plates
C] Converging plates
D] Middle portion
104] Which instrument is used to detect and record seismic waves?
A] Barograph
B] Seismograph
C] Diagraph
D] Hygrograph
105] Which is known as hypocenter?
A] Epicenter
B] Focus
C] Focal depth
D] Epicentral distance
106] What is the percentage of the structural cost of the building in the additional cost for the earthquake resisting structure?
A] About 1%
B] About 2%
C] About 3%
D] About 5%
107] What is the name of the part marked as 'X'?

A] Attachment plates
B] Lead plug
C] Rubber layer
D] Stiffening plates

108] What is the minimum distance to be maintained for the door opening from the cross wall? A] End of the wall B] 300mm C] 500mm D] 1000mm

109] What is the minimum thickness for making R.C. Bands?

A] 25mm

B] 50mm

C] 75mm D] 100mm

110] What is the distance between two through stones?

A] 150 to 300mm

B] 300 to 450mm C] 450 to 600mm

D] 600 to 750mm

111] Which one of the following in structure is the most important factors affecting its earthquake performance?

A] Workability

B] Serviceability

C] Flexibility

D] Responsibility

112] Which precaution should be taken for site selection to prevent earthquake?

A] Near unstable embankments

B] On sloping ground

C] Columns of different height

D] Continuity of subsoil

113] Which shape of building plan is safer for earthquake resisting building?

A] Square plan B] T- shaped plan

C] H- shaped plan

D] Plan have length morethan twice the width

114] What is the name of the part marked as 'X'?

A] Isolation bearings

B] Fixed base

C] Base

D] Isolated

115] What is the name of the figure?

A] Isolation bearings
B] Viscous damper
C] Friction damper
D] Yielding damper

116] Which device act like shock absorbers between the building and its foundation?

A] Damper
B] Spring
C] Base isolation
D] Air bag

117] Which isolation bearings are highly elastic?

A] Wood
B] Steel
C] Rubber
D] Bearing pads

118] Which material is strong in tensile strength?

A] Cement
B] Sand
C] Steel
D] Water

119] What kind of material is concrete?

A] Elasticity
B] Brittle
C] Stiff
D] Malleability

120] What is the maximum size of particle in fine aggregate?

A] 2.75 mm
B] 3.75 mm
C] 4.75 mm
D] 5.75 mm

121] What is the ratio for M15 grade of concrete?

A] 1]3]6

B] 1]2]4

C] 1]1.5]3

D] 1]1]2

122] What is the PH value of water is used for concrete?

A] 2 and 3

B] 4 and 5

C] 6 and 8

D] 9 and 10

123] What is the maximum absorption limit for coarse aggregate under water for 24 hours?

A] 3%

B] 5%

C] 7%

D] 9%

124] When does the probs of slab is removed if the span is more than 4.5 m?

A] 7 days

B] 14 days

C] 21 days

D] 28 days

125] What is the distance between two yokes in column formwork?

A] 0.50 m

B] 1.00 m

C] 1.50 m

D] 2.00 m

126] What is the name of the bar shown in figure?

A] Plain round bar

B] Twisted bar
C] Ribbed torsteel
D] Square bar
127] What is size marked as ’x‘?

A] 4d
B] 8d
C] 9d
D] 18d
128] What is the angle marked as ’x‘?

A] 15°
B] 30°
C] 45°
D] 60°
129] Which symbols denotes deformed bar?
A] ?
B] ?
C] #
D] @
130] What is the name of the part marked as ’x‘?

A] Steel plate
B] Steel bars
C] Reinforced bars
D] Mesh reinforcement

131] How many days the R.B slab is kept wet?

A] Two to four weeks

B] One to two weeks

C] One week

D] 3 days

132] Which type of beam has more than two supports?

A] Cantilever beam

B] Overhanging beam

C] Fixed beam

D] Continuous beam

133] What is the name of the beam shown in figure?

A] Simorted beam

B] Cantilever beam

C] Over hanging beam

D] Continuous beam

134] What is the shape of the bending moment diagram over the length of beam carrying a uniformly distributed load?

A] Linear

B] Cubical

C] Circular

D] Parabolic

135] What is the name of the load acting at a point?

A] Point load

B] Uniformly distributed load

C] Trapezoidal load

D] Triangular load

136] What kind of labour is required for erection of RCC structures compared to steel structures?

A] Less skilled

B] Semi skilled

C] Fully skilled

D] No skilled

137] Which of following is the advantage of reinforced concrete?

A] Low maintenance cost

B] Low compressive strength

C] Low yield strength

D] Low shear strength

138] Which is the disadvantage of reinforced concrete?

A] Light weight

B] Low shrinkage

C] Low strength

D] Low maintenance cost

139] Which material is used to increase the tensile strength in concrete?

A] Mud

B] Brick bats

C] Quarry dust

D] Steel

140] What is the grade of concrete for the concrete mix proportion is 1]1.5]3?

A] M 10

B] M 15

C] M 20

D] M 25

141] What is the concrete mix proportion for M10?

A] 1]3]6

B] 1]2]4

C] 1]1.5]3

D] 1]1]2

142] What is the initial cost of timber formwork compared to steel formwork?

A] Costly

B] Moderately

C] Cheap

D] Very low

143] Which part of building, the clear cover 25 mm or dia of bar whichever is more is used?

A] Beam

B] Column

C] Slab

D] Foundation

144] What is mass of 10 mm dia of steel bar per meter?

A] 0.302 kg

B] 0.395 kg

C] 0.617 kg D] 0.888 kg

145] Which type of reinforcement 6 mm diameter mild steel bars are used in walls?

A] Vertical reinforcement

B] Longitudinal reinforcement

C] Horizontal reinforcement

D] Spiral reinforcement

146] Where the bending moment is always zero?

A] At supports

B] At mid span

C] At 1/5 of span

D] At 1/7 of span

147] Which point of contraflexure occurs in the section?

A] Bending moment is maximum

B] Bending moment is zero or sign changes

C] Shear force is maximum

D] Shear force is minimum

148] Which condition the cracking occurs in concrete?

A] Chilling

B] Windy

C] Humidity

D] Milder climate

149] Which reinforcement is used for work of large dimensions, like massive foundation etc.? A] Rolled steel beams

B] Fabric made by welding

C] Square mesh

D] Square bars

150] Which material is coated at all the faces of concrete mould?

A] Water

B] Sand

C] Crude oil

D] Glue

151] What is the permissible stress for grade Fe 500?

A] 0.33 fy
B] 0.44 fy
C] 0.55 fy
D] 0.66 fy
152] Name of the apparatus.

A] Vicat's needle
B] Slump cone
C] Vibrating table
D] Cylindrical moulds
153] What is the recommended slump for R.C.C work?
A] 25 to 50 mm
B] 40 to 50 mm
C] 80 to 150 mm
D] 90 to 100 mm
154] What is the name of the part marked as 'x'?

A] Lateral ties
B] Spiral reinforcement
C] Vertical main steel
D] Cover

155] Which RCC member, bridges two or more walls or columns and supports the structural member coming over it?

A] Beam

B] Column

C] Footing

D] Slab

156] What is the minimum number of main bars are provided for transverse reinforcement? A] Two

B] Three

C] Four

D] Five

157] Which direction in one way slab the main reinforcement is provided?

A] Transverse

B] Length

C] Width

D] Depth

158] What is the maximum diameter of reinforcing bars to the total thickness of slab?

A] 1/5 B] 1/7

C] 1/8

D] 1/10

159] Which slab is supported on all four edges and the ratio of long span to short span is not more than two?

A] One way slab

B] Two way slab

C] Continuous slab

D] Cantilever slab

160] Name the reinforcement provided to counteract the tensional stress developed at corners of slab?

A] Main reinforcement

B] Torsion reinforcement

C] Singly reinforcement

D] Doubly reinforcement

161] How many vertical bars (minimum number) are provided for circular column?

A] Four B] Six

C] Eight

D] Ten

162] Which of the following method is used for super structure component?

A] Volumetric or modular construction

B] Brick slip

C] Rain screen

D] Render system

163] Which of the following option is taken, if the phone line system will be jammed after earth quake?

A] Text messages

B] Call loudly

C] Call through phone

D] Whats app call

164] Which of the following operation need to be done during earthquake?

A] Standing near the window

B] Collet and put together an emergency kit

C] Check your gas lines

D] Cover and hold on under a desk/tabl

165] What will be the compressive strength of 15cm cube after 28 days for a ordinary concrete of grade M30?

A] 30 N/mm2

B] 36 N/mm2

C] 40 N/mm2

D] 53 N/mm2

166] Which reinforcement strength is preferred in R.C.C?

A] Low tensile strength

B] High tensile strength

C] Bond strength

D] Compressive strength

167] What is the name of figure shown?

A] Twin twisted bar

B] Ribbed for steel

C] Grip bar D] Plain bar

168] Which bar the hooks are provided?

A] Plain bars

B] Hot rolled deformed bars

C] Cold twisted bars

D] Hard - drawn steel wire

169] What is the percentage reduction of strength for the 6 month old cement?

A] 20%

B] 30%

C] 40%

D] 50%

170] What is the total quantity of coarse and fine aggregate for 50kg cement for M15 grade of concrete required?

A] 625 kg

B] 480 kg

C] 330 kg

D] 250 kg

171] What is the compressive strength of 150 mm cube at 28 days ordinary concrete of grade M20?

A] 15 N/mm2

B] 20 N/mm2

C] 25 N/mm2

D] 30 N/mm2

172] Which type of cement available in three grades should be used for house construction? A] Ordinary portland cement

B] Rapid hardening portland cement

C] Portland slag cement D] High strength ordinary portland cement

173] What is the clear cover for foundation slabs and beams?

A] 15 mm

B] 25 mm

C] 40 mm

D] 50 mm

174] What is the density of steel?

A] 75.8 q/m^3

B] 78.5 q/m^3

C] 85.7 q/m^3

D] 87.5 q/m^3

175] What is name of the retaining wall?

A] Gravity retaining wall
B] Semi gravity retaining wall
C] Counter fort retaining wall
D] Cantilever retaining wall
176] What is the name of the part marked as 'x'?

A] Heel
B] Toe
C] Stem
D] Weep hole
177] Which structure is constructed for the purpose of retaining earth or other materials like coal, ore, water etc.?
A] Load bearing wall
B] Non load bearing wall
C] Retaining wall
D] Wing wall
178] What is the name of the part marked as 'x'?

A] Column support
B] Bitumen filler
C] Hinge reinforcement
D] Foundation

179] What is the name of the structure in which components such as beam, column and footing are monolithic in design and construction?

A] Portal frame
B] Non-portal frame
C] Rigid frame
D] Gabled frame

180] What is name of the structure?

A] R.C.C framed structure
B] Rigid frame structure
C] Braced frame structure
D] Portal frame structure

181] What is the name of the frame structure?

A] Portal frame with hinge base
B] Portal frame with fixed base
C] R.C.C framed structure

D] Portal frame

182] Which diameter of reinforcement bars are used for heavy foundations, large girders or counterforts?

A] 20 mm

B] 25 mm

C] 32 mm

D] 40 mm

183] Which type of mixer used for large quantity of concrete?

A] Hand mixing

B] Batch mixing

C] Tilting drum mixers

D] Continuous mixer

184] Where does covering of render is used?

A] Roof

B] Floor

C] Outside of the building

D] Inside of the building

185] What is length of one 'U' type hook?

A] 4?

B] 8?

C] 9?

D] 18?

186] What is the excess length of the one side of the cranked bar?

A] 0.212 d

B] 0.414 d

C] 0.616 d

D] 0.818 d

187] What is the weight / m of 12 mm diameter round bar?

A] 0.39

B] 0.62 kg/m

C] 0.89 kg/m

D] 1.58 kg/m

188] What is the name of the truss marked as 'x'?

A] Plate girder railway bridge

B] Lattice tower
C] Steel chimney
D] Warron truss used in bridges
189] What is the name of the steel section?

A] H - section
B] I - section
C] T - section
D] Z - section
190] What is the name of part marked as 'x'?

A] Main beam
B] Secondary beam
C] Web cleats
D] Seat angles
191] What is the name of the part marked as 'x'?

A] Cement concrete base
B] Base plate
C] Cleat angle
D] Gusset plate
192] What is the name of the connection?

A] Framed connection
B] Seated connection
C] Column to beam framed connection
D] Column to beam seated connection
193] What is the name of the connection?

A] Framed connection

B] Column to beam connection
C] Seated connection
D] Steel stanchion
194] Which span the plate girders are used?
A] More than 5 m
B] More than 10 m
C] More than 15 m
D] More than 20 m
195] What is name of the part marked as 'x'?
A] Clearance
B] Flange
C] Stiffners
D] Packing plate
196] Which member carries mainly tensile force?

A] Tension
B] Beams
C] Plates
D] Torsion
197] What is the name of the section?

A] Tension members
B] Compression members
C] Torsion members

D] Beams

198] How much the diameter of the hole is larger than the nominal diameter of the rivet if it is less than or equal to 25 mm?

A] 0.5 mm

B] 1.0 mm

C] 1.5 mm

D] 2.0 mm

199] What is the name of rivet head?

A] Snap head

B] Pan head

C] Ellipsoidal head

D] Conical head

200] Which riveted joint consists of two parallel rows and rivets where rivets are just opposite each other?

A] Single riveted lap joint

B] Double riveted single lap joint

C] Double riveted single lap joint

D] Single cover butt joint

202] What is the name of the truss?

A] Fink truss

B] Fan truss

C] Compound fan truss

D] Compound fink truss

203] What advantage of cold former steel members over reinforced concrete and timber?

A] Termite - proof and rot proof

B] Economical

C] Shrinking and creeping at temperature

D] Less accurate detailing

204] What is the minimum distance between centres of any two adjacent rivet holes to the nominal diameter of the rivet?

A] 1.00 time

B] 1.50 times

C] 2.00 times

D] 2.50 times

205] What is the main advantage of structural steel?

A] High strength

B] Maintenance cost

C] Slowly erection

D] Fire proofing cost

206] What is the name of the water obtained from tube well?

A] Surface water

B] Sub-surface water

C] Ran-off

D] Potable water

207] What is the full form of P.H.E.?

A] Public Health Engineering

B] Plumbing Heating Electrical

C] Public Health Emergencies

D] Peer Health Educations

208] What is the name of the liquid flowing in sewer?

A] Sewer

B] Sewage

C] Sewerage

D] Storm water

209] What is the name of the water coming out of the kitchen, bathroom, wash basin?

A] Garbage

B] Sullage

C] Sewage

D] Discharge

210] Which factor does sanitaty sewage quantity directly depends on?

A] Rate of water supply

B] Area
C] Population
D] Precipitation
211] Which type of sewer system are preferred in India?
A] Partial
B] Combined
C] Direct
D] Separate
212] Which device is used to prevent sewer gased from entering the building?
A] Filter
B] Trap
C] Ventilator
D] Vacuum pump
213] What is the angle between the drains and inspection manhole?
A] 45°
B] 90°
C] 135°
D] 180°
214] Which pipeline is laid in buildings to take out the sewage under the ground?
A] Steps
B] Barrel
C] Down tank
D] Sewer
215] Which material is made by PVC pipes?
A] Steel
B] Plastic
C] Copper
D] Silver
216] Which type of trap is used in Indian water closet?
A] S trap
B] P trap
C] U trap
D] Gully trap
217] What is the first stage in sewage treatment process?
A] Sedimentation
B] Screening

C] Filteration

D] softening

218] What is the term for water inside trap which prevents gas from entering?

A] Drain water

B] Water seal

C] Waste water

D] Trap safety

219] What is the name of the appurtenance that are constructed at suitable intervals?

A] Manholes

B] Catch basin

C] Pumps

D] Sewer appurterance

220] What is the type of manhole having a depth greater than 1.5 m is called?

A] Straight manhole

B] Deep manhole

C] Shallow manhole

D] Normal manhole

221] What is the nominal shape of septic tank?

A] Square

B] Rectangle

C] Circular

D] Oval

222] Which material is used to make manhole cover?

A] Cast iron

B] Cement

C] Wood

D] Steel

223] What is the name for all kinds of liquid waste of a building?

A] Rubbish

B] Garbage

C] Ashes

D] Sewage

224] Which plumbing system is common in India?

A] One pipe system

B] Two pipe system

C] Single stack system

D] Single stack partially ventilated

225] Which pipe system of plumbing work soil and waste pipe are separated?

A] One pipe system

B] Two pipe system

C] Separate system

D] Combined system

226] How many chambers are there in a septic tank?

A] 2

B] 3

C] 4

D] 5

227] What should be the minimum diameter of the connecting pipe in the septic tank?

A] 60mm

B] 100mm

C] 300mm

D] 700mm

228] What is the maximum spacing of manhole sewer size upto 0.3 mf?

A] 20 m

B] 30 m

C] 45 m

D] 75 m

229] Which type of pump should be selected in order to pump the sewage from a septic tank to the water treatment system?

A] Vertical slump pump

B] Progressive cavity pump

C] Centrifugal pump

D] Screw pump

230] How does the intensity of rain is expressed?

A] cm/minute

B] cm/hour

C] cm/day

D] cm/week

231] Which gas is mainly produced in septic tank?

A] Oxygen

B] Nitrogen

C] Hydrogen
D] Hydrogen sulphide
232] What is the period for sludge digestion in normal conditions?
A] 10 days
B] 20 days
C] 30 days
D] 60 days
233] Which sewer resist sulphide corrosion?
A] Brick sewer
B] Cast iron sewer
C] R.C.C. sewer
D] Lead sewer
234] What is the average temperature of sewage in India?
A] 10°C
B] 15°C
C] 20°C
D] 25°C
235] What is the design of sewage treatment?
A] 5-10 years
B] 15-20 years
C] 30-40 years
D] 40-50 years
236] What is the extension for 3D modelling file?
A] 0.3d
B] 0.3dm
C] 0.3m
D] 0.3dmo
237] Which command allows you to change 2D drawing into 3D model?
A] 3D modelling
B] Extrude
C] C plan
D] Ortho
238] What is the full form of WCS?
A] Western Co- ordinate System
B] World Co- ordinate System
C] Wide Co -ordinate System
D] Wrong Co-ordinate System
239] How many types of 3D modelling are in AutoCad?

A] 1
B] 2
C] 3
D] 4

240] How many types of surfaces are in surface modelling?
A] 1
B] 2
C] 3
D] 4

241] Which command allows you to change the direction and origin of construction plane?
A] Plane
B] Splane
C] C- plane
D] O- plane

242] What is the shortcut for grid command?
A] F6
B] F7
C] F8
D] F9

243] What is the shortcut for polar?
A] F8
B] F9
C] F10
D] F11

244] What is the key for 3D OSNAP?
A] F1
B] F2
C] F3
D] F4

245] Which key is used to access shortcut command in IBM compatible computer?
A] Ctrl
B] Alt
C] Ctrl + Alt
D] Tab

246] What is the command used to toggle between isometric planes?
A] Ctrl + E

B] Ctrl + F

C] Ctrl+ G

D] Ctrl + H

247] What is the shortcut for design centre palatte?

A] Ctrl +1

B] Ctrl + 2

C] Ctrl+ 3

D] Ctrl + 4

249] What is the shortcut for rendering an image?

A] RS

B] RSP

C] RP

D] RW

250] What is the shortcut for rendering a specified part of drawing?

A] RB

B] RC

C] RD

D] RP

ANSWERS]

1]B; 2]B; 3]A; 4]A; 5]D; 6]A; 7]D; 8]D; 9]C; 10]B; 11]C; 12]A; 13]B; 14]B; 15]C; 16]C; 17]D; 18]B; 19]B; 20]B; 21]A; 22]B; 23]B; 24]A; 25]A; 26]C; 27]B; 28]B; 29]D; 30]C; 31]A; 32]B; 33]B; 34]A; 35]C; 36]A; 37]C; 38]B; 39]C; 40]B; 41]A; 42]C; 43]B; 44]C; 45]C; 46]B; 47]B; 48]C; 49]D; 50]B; 51]B; 52]B; 53]C; 54]B; 55]C; 56]A; 57]C; 58]C; 59]A; 60]A; 61]D; 62]C; 63]D; 64]C; 65]C; 66]C; 67]C ; 68]C; 69]B; 70]B; 71]B; 72]C; 73]C; 74]C; 75]C; 76]B; 77]C; 78]C; 79]C; 80]C; 81]C; 82]C; 83]B; 84]C; 85]A; 86]C; 87]D; 88]B; 89]B; 90]B; 91]B; 92]C; 93]A; 94]A; 95]C; 96]D; 97]D; 98]A; 99]C; 100]D; 101]B; 102]C; 103]A; 104]B; 105]B; 106]D; 107]C; 108]C; 109]C; 110]D; 111]C; 112]D; 113]A; 114]A; 115]B; 116]C; 117]C; 118]C ; 119]B ; 120]C ; 121]B ; 122]C ; 123]B ; 124]B ; 125]B ; 126]C ; 127]A; 128]C ; 129]C ; 130]D; 131]A; 132]A; 133]B ; 134]D; 135]A; 136]A; 137]A; 138]C ; 139]D; 140]C ; 141]A; 142]C ; 143]A; 144]C ; 145]B ; 146]A; 147]B ; 148]B; 149]A; 150]C; 151]C; 152]B; 153]C; 154]C; 155]A; 156]A; 157]C; 158]C; 159]B; 160]B; 161]B; 162]A; 163]A; 164]D; 165]A; 166]B; 167]A; 168]A; 169]B; 170]C; 171]B; 172]A; 173]D; 174]B; 175]D; 176]A; 177]C; 178]C; 179]A; 180]A; 181]B; 182]D; 183]D; 184]C; 185]C; 186]B; 187]C; 188]D; 189]C; 190]C; 191]B; 192]A; 193]D; 194]D; 195]C; 196]A; 197]B; 198]C; 199]A; 200]B; 201]D; 202]D; 203]A; 204]D; 205]A; 206]B;

207]A; 208]B; 209]B; 210]C; 211]B; 212]B; 213]D; 214]D; 215]B; 216]B; 217]B; 218]B; 219]A; 220]B; 221]B; 222]A; 223]D; 224]B; 225]B; 226]A; 227]B; 228]B; 229]C; 230]B; 231]D; 232]C; 233]D; 234]C; 235]C; 236]B; 237]B; 238]B; 239]C; 240]B; 241]C; 242]B; 243]C; 244]D; 245]B; 246]A; 247]B; 248]A; 249]C; 250]B;

1] Which system of transportation is the fastest and provides more comfort for men and material?

A] Railways

B] Airways

C] Waterways

D] Roadways

2] Which mode of transportation has the maximum flexibility for travel with respect to route, directions, time etc?

A] Roadways

B] Railways

C] Waterways

D] Airways

3] Where did the Central Road Research Institute Started?

A] England

B] Nagpur

C] New Delhi

D] France

4] When did the IRC was set up?

A] 1943

B] 1860

C] 1934

D] 1973

5] Who created central public works department to look after the work of road?

A] Lord William Bentick

B] Lord Mayo

C] Lord Dalhousie

D] Lord Ripon

6] Which cross slope is given to the top layer of road in Macadam Construction?

A] 1 in 20

B] 1 in 45

C] 1 in 10

D] 1 in 36

7] Which is the highest point of a cross section of highway?

A] 1 in 20

B] Sub base

C] Carriage way

D] Crown

8] What is the time required for a driver to realise the necessity of applying brakes to the vehicles?

A] Reaction

B] Reflection

C] Perception

D] Sight distance

9] Which alternative road is provided to divert traffic to avoid obstruction?

A] Loop

B] Ring

C] Trunk

D] By pass

10] What is marked as 'X'?

A] Right of way

B] Formation

C] Roadway

D] Carriage way

11] What is the width of shoulders in roads?

A] 0.5m to 1.25m

B] 1.25m to 2m

C] 2m to 4m

D] 4m to 6m

12] Which is the portion of the road constructed for vehicular traffic?

A] Right way

B] Formation

C] Carriage way

D] Road way

13] Which is the basic requirement of alignment?

A] Crosses maximum number of bridges

B] Short

C] Lengthy straight routes

D] Curves

14] What is the restriction given to lengthy straight routes while setting road alignment?

A] Minimum

B] Maximum

C] Depends on gradient

D] Depends on rise and fall

15] Which survey established the centre line of the actual highway?

A] Location

B] Preliminary

C] Reconnaissance

D] Cadasral

16] Which survey is conducted to find the number of possible alternative routes between two points?

A] Preliminary

B] Reconnaissance

C] Location

D] Detailed

17] Which is the classification of road according to importance?

A] State highways

B] Second class

C] Cement concrete

D] Express highways

18] What is the normal recommended land width of national highway in open area?

A] 24m B] 25m

C] 35m

D] 45m

19] Which road connects areas of production and market with state highways and railways? A] National highway

B] Major district

C] Village

D] Other district

20] What is the minimum width of shoulders provided in national highways?

A] 1m

B] 1.5m C] 2m

D] 2.5m

21] What is the value of camber provided in the carriage way of gravel road?

A] 1 in 30 to 1 in 35

B] 1 in 25 to 1 in 30

C] 1 in 15 to 1 in 20

D] 1 in 10 to 1 in 15

22] Which camber is provided for earth roads?

A] 1 in 25 to 1 in 30

B] 1 in 20 to 1 in 25

C] 1 in 5 to 1 in 20

D] 1 in 5 to 1 in 10

23] Which is the direction of rolling in highway construction?

A] Sides and proceeds to centre B] Centre and proceeds to sides

C] Centre only

D] One side and proceed to other

24] Which is an advantage of cement concrete pavement?

A] Initial coat is low

B] Tractive resistance is low

C] Rolling resistance is high

D] Less time for construction

25] What is the another name of continuous bay method?

A] Alternate

B] Strip

C] Expansion

D] Traverse

26] Which circular curve consists of a single arc of uniform radius?

A] Compound

B] Simple C] Reverse

D] Transition

27] How a simple circular curve designated?

A] Curvature of the curve

B] Radius of the curve

C] Angle substended by an arc

D] Angle substended by a chord

28] Which transition curve is recommended by the IRC in the horizontal alignment of highway?

A] Spiral

B] Lemniscate

C] Cubic parabola

D] Summit

29] Which instrument is used for setting out curves in angular method?

A] Compass

B] Tape

C] Chain

D] Theodolite

30] Which is the linear method of setting out a simple circular curve?

A] Successive bisection of arcs

B] Two theodolite method

C] Tachometric method

D] Rankin's method

32] How much extra width of pavement on horizontal curves is given for a radius of 21 to 40m for two lane?

A] 1.5m

B] 1.2m

C] 0.9m

D] 0.6m

33] What is the minimum width provided for the cycle track in urban areas?

A] 1m

B] 1.5m

C] 2m

D] 3m

34] What is the minimum shoulder width recommended by IRC?

A] 1.30m

B] 1.85m

C] 2m

D] 2.5m

35] What is the value of minimum gradient?

A] 1 in 14.3

B] 1in 20

C] 1in 30

D] 1 in 200

36] What is the minimum sight distance recommended by IRC for minor roads?

A] 11m

B] 15m

C] 18m

D] 20m

37] What is the main purpose of providing camber?

A] To follow IRC specification

B] To prevent entry of moisture into subgrade

C] To maintain equilibrium

D] To follow specifications

38] Which shape of the surface drain is most preferred for heavy discharge in road?

A] Rectangular

B] U shaped

C] Semicircular

D] V shaped

39] Which culvert is used if the water opening is less than 15m^2 and road crosses the water way on a relatively high embankment?

A] Pipe

B] Arch

C] Box

D] Slab

40] Which drain is suitable for small streets of less discharge?

A] V shaped

B] Semi circular

C] Rectangular

D] U shaped

41] What is the rise in level of the river water due to obstruction of bridge?

A] Highest flood level

B] Run off

C] Afflux

D] Free board

42] Which is the intermediate support of a bridge superstructure?

A] Foundation

B] Pier

C] Abutment

D] Wing wall

43] Which is the temporary pier made in the river bed?

A] Kerb

B] Scuppers

C] Afflux

D] Cribs

44] What is the minimum distance between the specified position on a bridge?

A] Bearings

B] Clearance

C] Afflux

D] Water way

45] Which foundation is suitable for the construction of bridge?

A] Pile

B] Shallow

C] Grillage

D] Inverted arch

46] Which material is suitable for caisson of open well type?

A] Cast iron

B] RCC

C] Steel

D] Timber

47] Which is a temporary structure constructed to remove water or soil from an area to carry construction under dry condition?

A] Caisson

B] Well

C] Coffer dam

D] Box

48] Which is most common type of coffer dam?

A] Wells

B] Dike

C] Pneumatic

D] Box

49] What is the shape of the wingwall if it is inclined in plan?

A] Straight

B] Return wall

C] Square

D] Splayed

50] What is the name of the abutment shown in figure?

A] Straight
B] Splayed wing wall
C] Return wing wall
D] Straight wing wall
51] What is the name of the wingwall if the angle of splay 90°?
A] Splayed
B] Return
C] Straight
D] Tee abutment
52] Which bridge composed of several small spans for crossing a valley?
A] Aqueduct
B] Fort
C] Viaduct
D] Deck
53] What is the maximum span of culvert?
A] 2 m
B] 3 m
C] 5 m
D] 6 m
54] Which bridge is mostly used for railway bridges of small spans?
A] Steel girder
B] Steel trough plate
C] Suspension
D] Steel truss
55] Which bridge is shown in figure?

A] Semi through
B] Deck
C] Through
D] Suspension
56] What is marked as 'x'?

A] Clearance
B] Approach
C] Free board
D] Apron
57] Which is the main characteristic for an ideal site for a bridge?
A] Stream should be broad
B] Built up areas
C] Reach of stream should be straight
D] Whirls and cross currents
58] What plays a great role in fixing the height of bridge?
A] Design
B] Effect of scouring
C] Highest flood level
D] Type of traffic
59] Which is provided for the superstructure in the alignment on curve in hilly areas?
A] RCC girders

B] Box culverts

C] Dumb bell pier

D] Column bents

60] When did spread foundation is adopted for bridges?

A] Good soil is available at shallow depth

B] Depth of water is more

C] Good soil is not available at shallow depth

D] Tension developed is more

61] Which foundation is adopted when the loose soil extends to a great depth?

A] Spread

B] Raft

C] Caisson

D] Pile

62] Which foundation is provided for heavy works at a depth of 12 m to 15 m below the level of standing water surface?

A] Well

B] Caisson

C] Coffer dam

D] Pile

63] Which caisson the ratio of sinking effort to skin friction is maximum?

A] Circular well

B] Box

C] Dumb well

D] Pneumatic caisson

64] What is the minimum percentage of oxygen concentration in underground air quality for tunnel?

A] 12.5’%

B] 15.5‘%

C] 17.5’%

D] 19.5‘%

65] What is the maximum noise levels of ventilation fans while measure at the closest point of employee exposure?

A] 90 decibel

B] 100 decibel

C] 120 decibel

D] 130 decibel

66] Who started the development of railways in India?

A] George stephenson

B] Lord dalhousie

C] Lord curzon

D] Lord ripon

67] Which gauge is adopted for main cities and routes of maximum intensities?

A] Broad

B] Narrow

C] Metre

D] Wide

68] What is the process for filling the ballast around the sleepers?

A] Creep

B] Turn table

C] Boxing

D] Coning

69] What is the width of broad gauge?

A] 0.16 m

B] 0.762 m

C] 1.00 m

D] 1.676 m

70] What is the name for raising of the level of the outer rail over that of inner rail?

A] Creep

B] Cant

C] Boxing

D] Wearing

71] What is the name of the defect in rail due to abnormality of heavy load?

A] Hogging

B] Wear

C] Creep

D] Kink

72] What is the length of bull headed rail?

A] 16.7 m

B] 18.29 m

C] 18.6m

D] 19.2mm

73] What is the name of the steel placed end to end to provide a level surface for the movement of trains?

A] Ballast

B] Sleepers

C] Rails

D] Fish plates

74] What is the minimum depth of ballast for broad gauge?

A] 20 cm

B] 30 cm

C] 40 cm

D] 50 cm

75] What is the minimum spacing between sleepers in broad gauge?

A] 200 mm

B] 250 mm

C] 300 mm

D] 500 mm

76] Which is a cast iron sleeper?

A] Duplex

B] Steel

C] Pot

D] Box

77] What is the standard size of ballast for wooden sleepers?

A] 25 mm

B] 40 mm

C] 50 mm

D] 60 mm

78] What is used for fixing the rails to the wooden sleepers?

A] Spikes

B] Bearing plates

C] Fish bolt

D] Rail chair

79] Which is used for changing the direction of engine?

A] Rail joint

B] Turn table

C] Points and crossing

D] Terminal station

80] Which is used for joining the rail?

A] Spikes

B] Rail chairs

C] Fish plates

D] Bearing plate

81] What is the defect of rail with its end or ends bent in vertical direction?

A] Wear of rails

B] Hogging of rails

C] Creep of rails

D] Bending of rails

82] Which direction does rail creep occurs?

A] Longitudinal

B] Lateral

C] Vertical

D] Transverse

83] Which is used to reduce creeping of rail?

A] Bearing plates

B] Spikes

C] Anchors

D] Chairs

84] Which method is used to repair the worn out or damaged rails and to built up damaged components of points and crossing?

A] Bending

B] Hogging

C] Creep

D] Welding

85] Which area wear of rails maximum?

A] Top of rail

B] End of rail

C] Inner side of rail

D] Head of rail

86] What is the height of embankment above HFL in the construction of permanent way?

A] 30 cm

B] 50m

C] 60 cm

D] 65 cm

87] What is the process of tightly ramming the ballest under the sleepers to transmit the load?

A] Packing
B] Laying
C] Boxing
D] Fixing
88] What is the name of the spike is in figure?

A] Round
B] Screw
C] Elastic
D] Dog
89] Which warner signal is first seen by the driver in railway station?
A] Disc signal
B] Home signal
C] Outer signal
D] Routing signal
90] Which crossing the right hand rail of one track crosses the left hand rail of another track and vice versa?
A] Acute angle
B] Obtuse angle
C] Square
D] Rectangular
91] Which underground water nourishes the plant roots by capillarity?
A] Subsurface
B] Surface
C] Flood
D] Flow
92] Which method of irrigation is called trickle irrigation?
A] Furrow
B] Sprinkler
C] Drip
D] Border strip

93] What is the main advantage of irrigation?

A] Water logging

B] Yield of crops

C] Complex

D] Damper climate

94] Which irrigation method water is supplied to lower level by the action of gravity?

A] Flow

B] Lift

C] Sprinkler

D] Subsurface

95] Which crops are sown in autumn in harvested in spring?

A] Kharif

B] Autumn

C] Rabi

D] South west monsoon

96] What is the relation between duty (D) Delta (?) and base period (B)?

A] ? = (86.4B / D)

B] ? = (864B / D)

C] ? = (8.64B / D)

D] ? = (8640B / D)

97] What is the time between first watering of a crop on sowing to its last watering before harvesting?

A] Base period

B] Rabi season

C] Kor period

D] Crop period

98] What is the total depth of water required by a crop during the entire period in the field?

A] Duty

B] Base period

C] Delta

D] Crop period

99] What is the first watering before sowing the crop?

A] Kor watering

B] Paleo

C] Delta

D] Duty

100] Which is the graphical representation of average rainfall between rainfall excess?

A] Hyetograph

B] Hydrograph

C] S-hydrograph

D] Unit hydrograph

101] Which catchment area run off will be more?

A] Fan shaped

B] Tree shaped

C] Fern shaped

D] Circular

102] Which is the angle that the axis of head regulator makes with the axis of the weir?

A] 90° to 120°

B] 90° to 60°

C] 90° to 100°

D] 180°

103] Which construction is at the head of the canal to divert the river water towards the canal?

A] Storage head work

B] Diversion head work

C] Barrage

D] Weir

104] Which is called safety valve of a dam?

A] Drainage gallary

B] Inspection gallary

C] Spill way

D] Outlet sluices

105] What is the name for accumulation of water in the form of an artificial lake?

A] Spill ways

B] Barrages

C] Reservoir

D] Groynes

106] What is the classification of dam based on use?

A] Detention

B] Debris

C] Rigid

D] Buttress

107] Which of the following is non rigid dam?

A] Concrete

B] Rock fill

C] Gravity

D] Arch

108] Where did the surplus water in weir is allowed to flow?

A] Gates

B] Crest

C] Spill way

D] Openings

109] What is the life period of thermal plant?

A] Less than 30 years

B] More than 30 years

C] Less than 50 years

D] More than 50 years

110] What is marked as 'x'?

A] Turbine

B] Draft tube

C] Gallery

D] Pen stock

111] Which irrigation constant and continuous supply of water is assured throughout the crop period?

A] Flood

B] Artificial

C] Perennial

D] Inundation

112] Which crop is grown at a particular crop season?

A] Culturable cultivated area

B] Gross commanded area

C] Culturable commanded area

D] Culturable incultivated area

113] When does hydrograph called as unit hydrograph?

A] 1 cm of runoff from rainfall

B] 3 cm of runoff from rainfall

C] 1 mm of runoff from rainfall

D] 3 mm of runoff from rainfall

114] What is the unit for measuring rainfall?

A] cm

B] mm

C] Feet

D] No unit

115] Which is the main function of diversion head work of a canal?

A] To remove silt

B] To control floods

C] To store water

D] To raise water level

116] Which is provided in the diversion headwork to scour away silt deposited?

A] Fish lader

B] Groynes

C] Barrage

D] Under sluices

117] Which is the main factor for selection of site for a reservoir?

A] Maximum runoff

B] Maximum percolation

C] Wide opening

D] Minimum runoff

118] What is the name of dam?

A] Rock fill dam
B] Concrete buttress dam
C] Earth dam
D] Combined Earth and Rock dam

119] Which is known as spill way?
A] Water spread dam
B] Detention dam
C] Debris dam
D] Over flow dam

120] Which is the sheet of over flowing water?
A] Head
B] Nappe
C] Upstream
D] Crest

121] What is the name of the structure placed in river to increase the depth of water?
A] Barrage
B] Weir
C] Notch
D] Crest

122] What is the name of the impervious barrier constructed across a perennial river to raise the water level on the upstream side?
A] Barrage
B] Weir
C] Notch
D] Mouth piece

123] Which element of hydroelectric power plant reduce the water hammer pressure formed in the penstock?
A] Valves
B] Surge tank
C] Turbines
D] Draft tubes

124] Which canal is constructed to feed two or more canals?
A] Carrier
B] Feeder
C] Navigation
D] Irrigation

125] Which of the following canal is classified based on nature of supply?

A] Carrier

B] Feeder

C] Navigation

D] Permanent

126] Which canal carries water for another canal besides doing irrigation?

A] Carrier

B] Feeder

C] Navigation

D] Power

127] What is marked as 'X'?

A] Free board

B] Canal bed

C] Berm

D] Bank

128] Which canal is aligned along a water washed?

A] Contour

B] Side slope

C] Ridge

D] Power

129] Which canal is also known as ridge canal?

A] Contour

B] Watershed

C] Side slope

D] Main

130] What is marked as 'X'?

A] Free board
B] Canal bed
C] Berm
D] Bank
131] What is also known as canal fall?
A] Canal syphon
B] Canal drop
C] Super passage
D] Aqueduct
132] What is marked as 'X'?

A] Distributory head regulator
B] Off take channel
C] Parent canal
D] Cross regulator
133] What is marked as 'X' ?

A] Parent canal
B] Silt jetty
C] Off take canal
D] Cross regulator
134] Which cross drainage work is constructed to carry canal over drainage?

A] Aqueduct
B] Super passage
C] Canal syphon
D] Level crossing

135] Which cross drainage work is constructed to carry canal below drainage?

A] Aqueduct
B] Super passage
C] Level crossing
D] Inlet

136] Which cross drainage work is constructed to cross the canal and drainage at the same level?

A] Aqueduct
B] Super passage
C] Canal syphon
D] Level crossing

137] What is marked as 'X'?

A] FSL
B] Stream
C] HFL
D] Canal

138] What is marked as 'X'?

A] Canal syphon

B] Drainage

C] Culvert

D] Trough

139] What is the name given to built up area of building measured at floor level of any storey? A] Plinth area

B] Floor area

C] Circulation area

D] Carpet area

140] What is the name given to area of a building consisting of verandah's, passages, corridors, balconies etc.?

A] Circulation area

B] Horizontal circulation area

C] Vertical circulation area

D] Carpet area

141] What percentage of plinth area is provided for horizontal circulation area?

A] 5 to 10%

B] 10 to 15%

C] 15 to 20%

D] 20 to 25%

142] What percentage of plinth area of the residential building comes to carpet area?

A] 40 to 55%

B] 50 to 65%

C] 60 to 75%

D] 70 to 85%

143] What percentage of estimate cost is charged for centage charges?

A] 5 to 10%

B] 10 to 15%

C] 15 to 20%

D] 20 to 25%

144] Which is rough cost estimate?

A] Revised estimate

B] Annual repair estimate

C] Plinth area estimate

D] Supplementary estimate

145] Which is an item rate estimate?

A] Plinth area
B] Annual repair
C] Cubical content
D] Preliminary
146] What is the sequence of booking measurements?
A] Breadth, length and depth
B] Number, length and depth
C] Diameter, length and density
D] Length, breadth and height
147] What is the minimum length for bill quantity calculation?
A] 0.5 mm
B] 1 mm
C] 1cm
D] 10 cm
148] What is the minimum area for bill quantity calculation?
A] 1 mm^2
B] 1 cm^2
C] .01 sq.m
D] 1m^2
149] What is the unit for excavation in M.K.S system?
A] m
B] sq.m^2
C] cu.m
D] No
150] What is the minimum cubical quantity for bill quantity calculation?
A] 1 mm^3
B] 1 cm^3
C] 0.01 m^3
D] 0.1 m^3
151] What is the unit for cement concrete in M.K.S. system?
A] Nos.
B] m
C] sq.m
D] cu.m
152] What is the unit for brick work in cement mortar for superstructure in MKS system?
A] m
B] sq.m

C] cu.m

D] Nos.

153] What is the unit for steel reinforcement bars etc in RCC, RB work in MKS system?

A] m

B] Nos.

C] Quintal

D] sq.m

154] What is the unit for ridges, valleys, gutters in M.K.S system?

A] metre

B] sq.m

C] cu.m

D] Nos.

155] What is the unit for flooring in MKS system?

A] m

B] sq.m

C] cu.m

D] Nos.

156] What is the minimum lead for earth work excavation?

A] 10 m

B] 20 m

C] 30 m

D] 50 m

157] What is the minimum lift for earthwork excavation?

A] 1 m

B] 1.5 m

C] 2.0 m

D] 3.0 m

158] What is the measuring unit for soling layer?

A] m

B] sq.m

C] cu.m

D] Nos.

159] How much area of the opening is ignored for the masonry quantity calculation?

A] 1. sq.cm

B] 10 sq.cm

C] 100 sq.cm

D] 1000 sq.cm

160] What is the measuring unit for cornice?

A] m

B] sq.m

C] cu.m

D] mm

161] What is the measuring unit for modern door and window frames?

A] m

B] sq.m

C] cu.m

D] mm

162] What is the scale range used for the preparation of layout plan?

A] 1cm = 5m to 1cm = 10m

B] 1cm = 10m to 1cm = 20m

C] 1cm = .5km to 1cm = 1km

D] 1cm = 5km to 1cm = 10km

163] Which data is necessary for the preparation of estimate?

A] Labour

B] Material

C] Fund

D] Drawings

164] Which estimate is prepared while the expenditure on a work exceeds by more than 10%? A] Supplementary

B] Revised

C] Annual repair

D] Cubical content

165] Which estimate is prepared while the original sanctioned estimate is exceeded by more than 5%?

A] Supplementary

B] Extension and improvement

C] Revised

D] Plinth area

166] Which estimate is required for administrative sanction?

A] Approximate

B] Detailed

C] Revised

D] Supplementary

167] How aggregate is specified?

A] Size in mm
B] Length in mm
C] Height and breadth in cm
D] Length in m, section in mm
168] Which brick wall thickness is measured in sq.m?
A] 10 cm
B] 15 cm
C] 20 cm
D] 30 cm
169] Which brick structure is measured in sq.m?
A] Reinforced brick work
B] Broken glass coping
C] Concrete fencing posts
D] Brick work in arches
170] What (%) percentage of steel work is provided for rivets in steel roof truss?
A] 3%
B] 5%
C] 7%
D] 10%
171] What is the density of mild steel?
A] 0.785 q/cu.m
B] 7.85q/cu.m
C] 78.5q/cu.m
D] 785q/cu.m
172] What is the plastering area for a pillar?
A] Length x breadth x height
B] Section area x height
C] Perimeter
D] Perimeter x height
173] What (%) percentage is added as contingencies in approximate estimate?
A] 1% to 5%
B] 5% to 10%
C] 10% to 12%
D] 10% to 15%
174] What is the out-turn of mason constructing stone arch work?
A] 0.40 cu.m

B] 0.55 cu.m

C] 0.80 cu.m

D] 0.90 cu.m

175] What is the out-turn of mason, constructing superstructure with brick masonry?

A] 0.55 cu.m

B] 0.85 cu.m

C] 1.00 cu.m

D] 1.25 cu.m

176] What percentage contractors profit is included in the analysis of rate?

A] 5

B] 10

C] 15

D] 20

177] What quantity bitumen is required for $100m^2$ first coat painting on DPC?

A] 75 kg

B] 100 kg

C] 125 kg

D] 150 kg

178] What quantity of stone is required for $1m^3$ of rubble masonary?

A] 0.5 cu.m

B] 0.75 cu.m

C] 1.00 cu.m

D] 1.25 cu.m

179] How many nominal size bricks are required for $1m^3$ of brick work?

A] 500

B] 600

C] 700

D] 800

180] What quantity of coarse aggregate is required for $100m^3$ of 1]2]4 cement concrete?

A] 84 m^3

B] 86 m^3

C] 88 m^3

D] 90 m^3

181] What is printed list of rates of various items of work maintained by the engineering department?

A] Schedule of rates

B] Analysis of rates

C] Item rates

D] Market rates

182] Who prepares the schedule of rates?

A] Engineering department

B] Contractors

C] Private agencies

D] Government agencies

183] How many mazdoor or helper is required per mason for brickmark?

A] 1

B] 1.5 to 2

C] 3 D] 4

184] What is the process of determining the fair price or value of a property?

A] Valuation

B] Estimation

C] Fixation

D] Taxation

185] What is the value of dismantled material?

A] Salvage

B] Scrap

C] Market

D] Book

186] What is the amount a property can fetch from open market?

A] Scrap value

B] Salvage value

C] Market value

D] Book value

187] What is the annual periodic payment for repayment of the capital amount invested by a party?

A] Capital cost

B] Annuity

C] Depreciation

D] Outgoings

188] Which cement concrete proportion is used for damp proofing first class building?

A] 1]1.5]3

B] 1]2]4

C] 1]2]6

D] 1]4]8

189] What is the minimum height specified for first class building?

A] 3.3 m

B] 3.7 m

C] 3.8 m

D] 3.9 m

190] Which cement concrete proportion is used for damp proofing second class building?

A] 1]1.5]3

B] 1]2]4

C] 1]2]6

D] 1]4]8

193] What material is specified for the plinth of 1st class building?

A] First class brick work in cement mortar 1]6

B] Second class brick work in cement mortar

C] Third class brick work in cement mortar

D] Sum dried brick work in mud mortar

194] What is the area by trapezoidal rule?

A] 764.5 m^2

B] 770.5 m^2

C] 780.5 m^2

D] 790.5m^2

195] What is the area by Simpsons rule?

A] 717 m^2

B] 727 m^2

C] 959 m^2
D] 1090 m^2
196] What is marked as 'x'?

A] Optical plummet
B] Collimator
C] Data out connector
D] Bottom plate
197] What is marked as 'x'?

A] Objective lens
B] Collimator
C] Optical plummet
D] Data out connector
198] What is marked as 'x'?

A] Top Handle

B] Collimator

C] Optical plummet

D] Data out connector

199] Which instrument is a combination of EDM, electronic theodolite and micro processor?

A] Total Station

B] Tacheometer

C] Distomite

D] Tellurometer

200] Which program is used for erecting perpendicular line to base line?

A] Stake out

B] Free station

C] Reference line

D] Tie distance

201] Which program is used for setting out points?

A] Resection

B] Stake out

C] Reference line

D] Remote height

202] Which instrument is used to findout the co-ordinates of a reflection and at the same time measuring the vertical angles?

A] Auto level

B] Total station

C] Theodolite

D] Transmit theodolite

203] What is the name of measurement for distances taken to a prism on reflecting foil most accurate?

A] Precise measurement

B] Rapid measurement

C] Tracking measurement

D] Angle measurement

204] Which measurement reduces the measurement time to a prism between 0.5 and 1's for both phase shift and pulsed systems?

A] Precise measurement

B] Rapid measurement

C] Tracking measurement

D] Angle measurement

205] Which range can be obtained for a reflector less measurement taken with a phase shift system?

A] 50 m

B] 100 m

C] 150 m

D] 200 m

206] What is the formula for principle of operation of EDM?

A] Velocity = Time x Distance

B] Velocity = Time / Distance

C] Velocity = Distance x Time

D] Velocity = Distance / Time

207] What is the abbreviation for EDM in surveying?

A] Electronic Distance Measurement

B] Engineering Distance Measurement

C] Electro Discharge Maching

D] Electronic Direct Mailing

208] What is the shape of a single reflector prism?

A] Cube corner

B] Cuboid corner

C] Circular

D] Triangular corner

209] In which conditions, the LCD screen does not work?

A] Cold

B] Hot

C] Warm

D] Wind

210] Faulty temperature and pressure measurement occurs by which source of error in EDM? A] Personal

B] Instrumental

C] Natural

D] Environmental

211] What is marked as 'x'?

A] Replector height

B] Instrumental height

C] Height of collimation

D] Slope height

212] What is the name of the figure given below?

A] Rectangular and polar co-ordinates

B] Polar to cartesian co-ordinates

C] Rectangular co-ordinates

D] Polar co-ordinates

213] What is the name of the figure given below?

A] Rectangular and polar co-ordinates
B] Polar to cartesian co-ordinates
C] Rectangular co-ordinates
D] Polar co-ordinates
214] What is the name of the figure given below?

A] Rectangular and polar co-ordinates
B] Polar to cartesian co-ordinates
C] Rectangular co-ordinates
D] Polar co-ordinates
215] What is the formula to findout the sum of interior angles of a closed polygon traverse?
A] (n - 2) x 360°
B] (n + 2) x 360°
C] (n - 2) x 180°
D] (n + 2) x 180°
216] Which are dedicated to the particular instrument and can store and process surveying observation?
A] Data recorders
B] Pocket calculators
C] Field note books
D] Pen-drives
217] Which is fitted with a total station capable of storing 900 to 10000 points?
A] Memory card

B] Data recorder
C] Internal memory
D] Field computer
218] What is the advantage of Total Station?
A] The instruments costly
B] Does not provide field note
C] Direct observation of sum not possible
D] Greater accuracy in area computation
219] What is the disadvantage of Total Station?
A] Automation of old maps
B] Local language support
C] Full GIS creation
D] The instrument is costly
220] Which is the total station with latest technology?
A] Mechanical
B] Semi automatic
C] Manual
D] Automatic
221] Which program is used to determine polygonal distance?
A] Tie distance
B] Reference line
C] Free station
D] Resection
222] Which program is used to determine the position of new station with reference to two known points?
A] Free station
B] Tie distance
C] Remote height
D] Reference line
223] Where is data stored in Total Station?
A] Pen drive
B] Data card
C] Micro processor
D] External hardware
224] What is the advantage of using EDM?
A] Precise measurement of distance
B] Electronic batteries
C] Expensive

D] Accuracy affected by atmospheric condition

225] What is the disadvantage of using EDM?

A] Capable of measuring long distances

B] Precise measurement of distance

C] Accuracy affected by atmospheric conditions

D] Relectorless are single person operation

226] Which trigonometrical value is correct?

A] O/H = sin ß

B] A/H = sin ß

C] O/A = sin ß

D] H/O = sin ß

227] What is the sum of the interior angles of a closed polygon traverse that has of 8 sides?

A] 720°

B] 1080°

C] 1440°

D] 1800°

228] Where the open traverse is used?

A] Topographic survey

B] Layout of engineering works

C] Construction of pipelines

D] Property measurement

229] Which country developed the GPS?

A] USA

B] India

C] Russia

D] Italy

230] What is meant by GPS?

A] Global Processing System

B] Global Positioning System

C] Geographic Positional System

D] Geographic Processing System

231] What is the orbital height for GPS?

A] 10,00 km

B] 15,000 km

C] 20,180 km

D] 24,280 km

232] Which is the common choice of co-ordinate for specifying position?

A] Latitude, departure and elevation

B] Latitude, longitude and elevation

C] Northing, southing and easting

D] Southing, azimuths and elevation

233] What is the distance between the UTM grid lines on topomaps?

A] 100 m

B] 1000 m

C] 2000 m

D] 5000 m

234] Where the master control station of control segment located?

A] Hawaii

B] Colorado

C] Diego Garcia

D] Kwajalein

235] How many operational satellites are available in space segment?

A] 24

B] 28

C] 32

D] 36

236] Which segment of GPS consists of satellite?

A] Control

B] Space

C] User

D] Navigation

237] Which segment of GPS consists of receivers?

A] Control

B] User

C] Space

D] Navigation

238] What is an advantage of GPS survey?

A] High precision

B] Weather dependent

C] Night operation only

D] Site intervisibility required

239] Which is an application of GPS for visually impaired?

A] MOBIC

B] GIS

C] Ramchers

D] Navigation

240] Which is an application of GPS for visually impaired in India?

A] Marine GOS

B] Drishti

C] Ramchers

D] GIS

241] What is meant by the study of something without direct contact?

A] Remote sensing

B] Geographic information system

C] Tachometry

D] Ranging

242] What is marked as 'x'?

A] Target

B] Energy source

C] Sensor

D] Transmission

243] What is the practice of determining the geometric properties of objects from photographic images?

A] Photogrammetry

B] Positioning

C] Remote sensing

D] Orientation

244] What is the another name for exposure station?

A] Air station

B] Nadir point

C] Zenith point

D] Horizon point

245] What is an advantage of GPS survey?

A] Two dimensional

B] Three dimensional

C] Weather dependent

D] Only day tim operation

246] What is an advantage of digital signal?

A] High cost

B] Difficult to control

C] Noise immunity

D] Nigidity in response to design

247] What is the process of getting digital equivalent of analog signals for processing?

A] Data acquisition

B] Data processing

C] Image recognition

D] Pattern recognition

248] What is an advantage of digital over analog signal processing?

A] Digital system is difficult to reprogramme

B] Digital signal processing provides better control of accuracy

C] Digital signals are difficult to store without deterioration

D] More ancient signal processing algorithms can be used

249] What is the advantage of photogrammetry?

A] Weather dependent

B] Covers large area C] Costlier

D] Complex system

250] What is the advantage for in setup of instrument photogrammetry?

A] Heavy equipments needed

B] Weather dependent

C] Less time consuming

D] Costlier

ANSWERS]

1]B; 2]A; 3]C; 4]C; 5]C; 6]D; 7]D; 8]C; 9]A; 10]D; 11]B; 12]C; 13]B; 14]A; 15]A; 16]B; 17]B; 18]D; 19]B; 20]C; 21]B; 22]B; 23]A; 24]B; 25]B; 26]B; 27]B; 28]A; 29]D; 30]A; 31]B; 32]A; 33]C; 34]D; 35]D; 36]B; 37]B; 38]A; 39]D; 40]B; 41]C; 42]B; 43]D; 44]B; 45]A; 46]A; 47]C; 48]B; 49]D; 50]C; 51]B; 52]C; 53]D; 54]B; 55]C; 56]C; 57]C; 58]C; 59]A; 60]A; 61]D;

62]B; 63]A; 64]D; 65]A; 66]B; 67]A; 68]C; 69]D; 70]B; 71]B; 72]B; 73]C; 74]A; 75]D; 76]C; 77]C; 78]A; 79]B; 80]C; 81]B; 82]A; 83]C; 84]D; 85]B; 86]C; 87]A; 88]D; 89]C; 90]A; 91]A; 92]C; 93]B; 94]A; 95]C; 96]C; 97]A; 98]C; 99]B; 100]B; 101]A; 102]A; 103]B; 104]C; 105]C; 106]A; 107]B; 108]B; 109]A; 110]D; 111]C; 112]A; 113]A; 114]B ; 115]D; 116]D ; 117]A; 118]C; 119]D; 120]B; 121]A; 122]B; 123]B; 124]B; 125]D; 126]A; 127]B; 128]C; 129]B; 130]A; 131]B; 132]A; 133]B; 134]A; 135]B; 136]D; 137]B; 138]A; 139]A; 140]B; 141]B; 142]B; 143]B; 144]C; 145]B; 146]D; 147]B; 148]C; 149]C; 150]C; 151]D; 152]C; 153]C; 154]A; 155]B; 156]C; 157]B; 158]B; 159]D; 160]A; 161]C; 162]B; 163]D; 164]B; 165]C; 166]A; 167]A; 168]A; 169]B; 170]B; 171]C; 172]D; 173]B; 174]A; 175]C; 176]B; 177]D; 178]D; 179]A; 180]A; 181]A; 182]A; 183]B; 184]A; 185]B; 186]C; 187]B; 188]A; 189]B; 190]B; 191]B; 192]C; 193]A; 194]D; 195]B; 196]A; 197]B; 198]B; 199]A; 200]C; 201]B; 202]B; 203]A; 204]B; 205]B; 206]D; 207]A ; 208]A; 209]A; 210]A; 211]B; 212]A; 213]C; 214]D; 215]C; 216]A; 217]C; 218]D; 219]D; 220]D; 221]A; 222]A; 223]C; 224]A; 225]C; 226]A; 227]B; 228]C; 229]A; 230]B; 231]C; 232]B; 233]B; 234]B; 235]A; 236]B; 237]B; 238]A; 239]A; 240]B; 241]A; 242]C; 243]A; 244]A; 245]B; 246]C; 247]A; 248]B; 249]B; 250]C;

www.ingramcontent.com/pod-product-compliance
Ingram Content Group UK Ltd.
Pitfield, Milton Keynes, MK11 3LW, UK
UKHW021917190726
13853UKWH00002B/708